ONCE A WARRIOR

ONCE A
WARRIOR
WIRED FOR LIFE

**Bridget C. Cantrell, Ph.D.
and Chuck Dean**

Once a Warrior: Wired for Life
Copyright © 2007 Bridget C. Cantrell and Chuck Dean. All rights reserved.

Published by WordSmith Books, LLC, P.O. Box 68065, Seattle, WA 98168

Cover design by Suzanne Steel of *Hot Steel Design*
Edited by: Judith Wagner
Interior Design by Rhiannon Jackson

ISBN 978-0-615-14132-9

Cantrell, Bridget C.
    Once a Warrior: Wired for life/ Bridget C. Cantrell & Chuck Dean. - 1st ed. -- Seattle, WA : WordSmith Publishing 2005

    p. ; cm.
    ISBN-13 978-0-615-14132-9

    1. Post-traumatic stress disorder--Prevention. 2.Post-traumatic stress disorder--Treatment. 3.Combat--Psychological aspects. 4. Stress (Psychology) 5. Psychology, Military. 6.Veterans--Mental health. I. Dean, Chuck. II. Title.

Printed in the United States of America.

DEDICATION

Soon after the war was over, the USS Pennsylvania, a flagship that fought in every major WWII battle in the South Pacific, met its end at the hand of an atomic bomb.

As the warship went under a young sailor who survived those battles aboard her was not far away; he had been chosen as one to observe nuclear testing in the Southern Hemisphere. He watched as his ship and home for those long treacherous months, when the Japanese submarines did everything they could to put it on the bottom, went down as a relic of no further use.

This book is dedicated to that sailor, Charlie S. Cantrell, and his lifetime partner Carmen Cantrell, who stood by him as he made all the necessary adjustments back to civilian life.

Coming from rural Texas, Charlie had never eaten a piece of store-bought bread until he joined the U.S. Navy during WWII. Ironically he went on to become a master baker of fine bread and rolls that kept a battleship's crew smiling day in and day out as they made long cruises into combat.

His ship may not have returned with him from overseas but something else did. He came back with a duffle bag stuffed full of life-altering memories that he has lived with since. After serving honorably both during WWII and the Korean Conflict Charlie never once regretted his service or experiences, and went on to have a successful life as a civilian. Our hats are off to Charlie and Carmen, and the thousands of other couples like them who have succeeded in making the journey home.

A SPECIAL MESSAGE TO THE MILITARY

As with any book written for a military audience, proper honor and respect for your service is of paramount consideration. Since our intention was to keep this work an easy read and to-the-point, we chose to use some general terms in identifying particular units and branches of service. We know the importance of maintaining unit recognition and esprit de corps, and hope you understand that for the sake of content flow and simplicity, we have not specifically delineated between Army, Navy, Air Force, Marine Corps, Coast Guard, National Guard, or Enlisted Reserve. We have simply used the term "troops" or "warriors" to identify every person for his or her service and sacrifice. We wanted to brief you on this in advance in case we have inadvertently identified you with a branch of the Armed Forces in which you did not serve.

~~ Combat Operational Stress (COS) & Post-Traumatic Stress Disorder (PTSD) ~~

To date, perhaps more than a million U.S. troops have served in Iraq and Afghanistan since the War on Terror began. Tens of thousands have shown some signs of serious stress upon their return. Throughout this book you will not only read about some of these stress reactions, but you will also learn how to deal with and recognize many of the symptoms as they arise.

SPECIAL MESSAGE TO THE MILITARY

Warriors may or may not return home with what is diagnosed as "post-traumatic stress disorder" (PTSD). Many of the signs of PTSD can be construed for what military stress teams now call Combat Operational Stress (COS). It has been determined that every participant in a war zone *will* manifest some aspects of COS (i.e. hyper-alertness, anxiety, frustration, anger, confusion, intolerance of "stupid" behavior, sleep disruption, etc.). Some readjustment issues can be commonly expected but this does not confirm that an individual has PTSD. If these symptoms continue to worsen and interfere with the quality of your life, we urge you to take proper steps to get some advice, diagnosis, and support.

One of our primary intentions in writing *Once a Warrior: Wired For Life* is to help you recognize any issues that may have resulted from your tour of duty—and to help you see that you are not alone. We hope you use this book as a tool for needed insight into what is happening as you begin your journey home.

CONTENTS

...ABOUT FACE

"Boys with a normal viewpoint were taken from the fields and offices and factories and classrooms and put into the ranks. There they were remolded; they were made over; they were made to 'about face,' to regard murder as the order of the day. They were put shoulder to shoulder, and through mass psychology they were entirely changed. We used them for a couple of years and trained them to think nothing at all of killing or of being killed. Then suddenly, we discharged them and told them to make another 'about face.' This time they had to do their own readjusting without mass psychology, without officers' aid and advice, without nation-wide propaganda. We didn't need them any more. So we scattered them about without any speeches or parades. Many, too many, of these fine young boys are eventually destroyed mentally, because they could not make that final 'about face' alone." (Written between WWI and WWII...)

—Smedley D. Butler, Major General, USMC - 1936
Two-time winner, Congressional Medal of Honor

AUTHORS' PREFACE

Since General Butler wrote those words, many significant changes have taken place in our military, and the term "warrior" has truly taken on a new meaning in the 21st Century. His words, however, continue to ring loud and clear. We could think of no better quotation to accentuate the reality of what this book is about.

Today, it is not just our "boys" who go off to war, but mothers, sisters, aunts, and even grandmothers. The current war (OIF/OEF) is the first war in which so many women have been exposed to hostile fire while doing such a vast array of combat-related jobs. How women are affected during and after combat is just now starting to be explored, and is worthy of the many studies now taking place. Regardless of gender or combat occupation specialty, today's combatants all have one important bridge to eventually cross after their war is over...That is to come home.

Our previous book, "Down Range: To Iraq and Back," centered primarily on the combat-induced aspects of trauma, and the readjustment difficulties among returning troops and their loved ones. We spoke of how life itself permanently changes in the eyes of someone who is called to participate in war, and how a once safe world becomes transformed into a threatening expedition for newly released soldiers as they begin their journey from warrior to civilian.

Since writing that book we have talked with military personnel from all branches, some still active and some not. The challenges of getting their lives back to normal are unique and the commonalities regarding personal desires for their futures, and the ensuing frustrations, are such that we have found this book necessary.

Through those conversations and reviewing research studies it is evident that much more needs to be done with our returning military's reintegration program. As a caring society we cannot afford to neglect the fact that "welcome home, go back to work and forget the war" is no easy task. Helping our military men and women transition back from an adrenaline-fueled, tactically disciplined life, to the carefree and relaxed way of life that exists in civilian environments is a critical endeavor indeed, for both the individual and the nation.

First and foremost, we want to point out clearly that this book does not center on the negative effects war can have on a person while serving in the military. We have, however, found it necessary to include detailed information to help readers recognize behaviors and symptoms that can make a good return home difficult. Our thrust in writing it is to inform and equip both the returning troops and the civilian community with awareness of the *positive* aspects gained through the skills, knowledge, and experiences of serving in our country's armed forces.

To further clarify the focal point of this book, and circumvent any possible misunderstandings, "...Wired for Life" (our book's subtitle) has several meanings throughout this book. *Wired* in one sense means hyper, restless, agitated, and indicates that a person may have a "wire loose" and is not functioning properly. Our effort in "Once a Warrior..." is to highlight ways to turn negatives into positives, and "having things wired" also means that something (or someone) has been put together well and is working properly. It is our conviction that our highly trained military personnel have tremendous potential to achieve a happy and successful life after their war experiences once they are released from the service.

There are certainly many beneficial aspects to military life and training; we see them all the time as we meet some of our young troops who are returning home. It is these elements that we want to flush out in order to help you make the most of yourself. As with most good things, however, there is sometimes a disappointing downside.

When undertaking the process of switching from soldier to civilian, there may be some problematic effects from your military training and combat experiences. It is necessary to recognize and address these potentially unpredictable elements as soon as you can; otherwise, you may find it difficult to attain a happy and productive way of life. To help you avoid some key pitfalls we have visited and re-visited some of the effects of wartime experiences.

Over the years of counseling veterans from several different eras, I (Bridget) have seen first-hand the difficulties veterans struggle with. Most are severely challenged in sorting out and understanding their responses and reactions to life, especially those ingrained reactions that come as a result of their training and wartime duty. I have spent countless hours in my therapy practice helping veterans and their loved ones unravel the myriad of issues that military wartime service creates. On the other hand, as a war veteran and combat trainer, I (Chuck) know how much people change, and *are* changed, as they are prepared for war. Some of these changes are productive; but over time others have proven to be less useful when returning to civilian life.

In this work the importance of a soldier-to-civilian "retraining" program becomes apparent. We believe that our government needs to implement one immediately for our transitioning military when their service has concluded. A combat training program should not be considered complete, or wholly effective, unless it has an ending chapter designed specifically to assist ex-combatants make a full return to civilian life.

Currently, much time and energy is expended on training citizen-soldiers to fight for and maintain a strong national defense. Our combatants are precision trained on how to engage and eliminate enemy forces, and to survive some of the worst case scenarios imaginable. However, and history bears this out, when these same combatants return to civilian life many of those "worst-case scenarios" continue to prevail and result in negative consequences. Unbeknownst to a widely divergent civilian world the conditioned responses and mindsets of veterans can be exceptionally counterproductive, and it is in everyone's best interest that equal time and effort be placed on reversing the process that made them into warriors in the first place.

A good example of where we are coming from can be made by illustrating with an example from some military training. If suddenly you realize that you have marched yourself into the middle of a mine field, what do you do? The first drill you learn is to never panic and/or take off in every direction. This could get you, and those close to you, hurt. Instead, the safest course of action is to methodically retrace every footstep by placing your feet (precisely) in the prints you left, taking you back out of the danger zone. In short, rather than trying to *forget* your military training after you become a civilian again, (which is impossible to do anyway), why not make it work *for* you?

In this book we will discuss some ideas on how to make this possible. These thoughts and suggestions are certainly not exhaustive, and you may discover some methods of your own after reading it. We are hopeful this book will be a good starting point to get your mind set in the right direction.

With that said, in tandem we have combined "forces" again to bring you another set of tools to make healthy transitions after wartime service. One of us a writer who works directly with combat veterans as a clinician specializing in the treatment of post-traumatic stress disorder, and the other a war veteran and ex-combat instructor. We welcome you to yet another leg of your journey back home.

Bridget C. Cantrell, Ph.D. and Chuck Dean

CHAPTER ONE

FIREFIGHTS AND FIREWALLS

"For those who fight for it, life has a special flavor the protected will never know."

Over the years veterans have struggled to find words that describe certain aspects of their experiences. A friend who served in Vietnam once spoke the following words that resonate for all who served.

"After one of our first major operations, my friends and I wandered over to our usual hangout spot to talk like we always did; but something was different this time. I looked around our group and we had one less person. Then the next time we got a chance to go to our spot, again there was one less, and so on. Losing our friends one at a time made us distant...not wanting to be too close to anyone, so if someone died it wouldn't hurt so much. "It don't mean nothin'" was a common phrase we used every day almost like a mantra. Oh, it meant a lot, but we had to tell ourselves it didn't mean anything when something bad happened...but it always hurt just the same.

"Coming back to the States this distance was so ingrained in me (us) that I could not maintain a relationship with anyone for many years. I dared not show *any* emotions, lest it reveal the true hurt and vulnerability I really carried in my heart. So I became cold like a stone. In situations where normal people were soft and sensitive, I was frozen and incapable of expressing any feeling at all. To this day, I still find some things in life that I just have to settle for...and it 'don't mean nothin'."

For years when I (Chuck) came home from the Vietnam War, I wondered how I could ever get my life back, and was convinced that no one would ever understand what I had seen and done. How can anyone explain to someone who has never been in combat what it is like? How to convey all the ways people change in the course of surviving a war remains a mystery to every combatant who returns home.

Silence is *not* the better part of valor. Clamming up and figuring that it would just go away on its own was my first big mistake. I needed to talk about my experiences, but at the time I had no idea that when I got back to my hometown I would not be able to just pick up where I had left off. Experience over the years has confirmed that picking up that same life would not be so easy, and actually would be impossible to do. I had to settle for finding my own ways to compensate. As I reflect back, most were not good ways to make a healthy transition.

When returning warriors, and those waiting at home, finally see the reality that things are now different, and we must move on, it is then that they can begin to take positive steps in the transition of "coming home." In conjunction with this insight they must also begin to confront their personal "firewalls."

If you are familiar with computers you most likely have heard the term "firewall." A firewall protects a computer network from unwanted outside interference and threats. It is a program or configuration that simply blocks and filters information attempting to infiltrate via an Internet connection. Incoming information is flagged and shielded from entering through the connection. Putting up an emotional firewall is a mechanism that many people use to buffer pain. It is no more than a protective shield just like one installed on a computer system.

Our personal trauma "firewall" works to filter or block possible harmful information in similar ways. We string up emotional devices to form barriers between us and life around us. We use these barriers to filter what we want (or don't want) to receive. If we perceive that a person or circumstance is potentially harmful, confusing, or overwhelming then that information gets flagged and censored.

While in dangerous, or life threatening situations, "firewalls" work well and are a natural defense system that aids in our survival. The only problem is that when the danger (or trauma) is no longer present, these existing firewalls remain and can make life very confusing. With this system still activated we sometimes do not make conscious conclusions or determine correctly whether the threat is real or imagined. Needless to say, this shield or emotional barrier puts people and circumstances at a distance, causing detachment and a strain on relationships. So, the very mechanism we put in place to maintain control and protect ourselves in combat now works overtime to ever widen the gap between us and other people.

As an ex-trainer of combat troops I have wondered over the years how feasible it is for our government to re-train warriors to become civilians again. If it is possible, and I certainly believe it is, then why has it not been implemented? It seems like a critical supplement to any training program our troops undertake.

I asked one retired Marine colonel about this and I was amazed when he answered, "What a profound idea!" In light of his knowledge and experience as a career Marine officer, this response spoke loud and clear. It was evident that the concept of re-training our military to be conventional citizens again has never been a hot topic tossed around in the circles of war planners. (Why on earth would they want to spend time and energy on such a non-productive activity, anyway?). I suppose the subject is avoided in the same vein as telling warriors about the real possibility of getting a good case of post-traumatic stress disorder before going into combat...It would be a distraction and most likely reduce their effectiveness on the battlefield. So we settle for letting them find out about it the hard way...through lives carved out at home by the sharp cutting edges of mishap when it is all over.

This is one slant on life that I am very familiar with...from many sides and angles. I served from 1967 to 1969 as an Army drill instructor at Fort Ord, California. During that time of turn-on, tune-in and drop-out I had the unique experience of preparing thousands of recruits for the war in Vietnam. Many of these warriors-to-be were draftees, and mostly those who did not keep their grades up in the various California colleges (Berkley, etc.). As a result Uncle Sam called them up and demanded their time and sacrifice. Many of them happened to be out of the Haight-Ashbury hippy crowd. They, along with the kids who could not afford college at the time, reported to the Army repo depots around the country.

It was the days of rock concerts, psychedelic drugs and free love, and it was very unusual to find anyone of draft age who was not into peace, love, and anti-establishment ways of thinking. Only days and hours removed from a love-in or a campus peace and anti-war demonstration, many confused (and resistant) young Americans arrived by bus at Fort Ord, near Monterey, California to become soldiers. As a drill sergeant I greeted them, and trained them step-by-step for basic combat over the next eight weeks. The staggering lines of disheveled boys with long hair, love beads, barefoot and stoned, appeared to be anything but "soldier-material"—and I always had my job cut out for me.

In 1967, as a member of an Army training cadre, and a Vietnam War veteran fresh from the combat zone, my assignment was to train (or convince) some very reluctant trainees to pull the trigger on other human beings. This gruesome idea had its own peculiarities due to the unpopularity of a war that made little sense to any of them.

Each eight-week training cycle I pushed troops through the basics of surviving the routines and rigors of combat, and tried to prepare them for what was in store for them in the jungles and rice paddies half a world away. Not once while training them did I give any thought to the permanent effect this type of training would have on millions of Americans for decades to come. I can verify to you that training in our military is only half done when we graduate from the schools of prepared instruction. The other half, and the half that really matters, is done via "O.J.T" (on-the-job-training). It is this "hands-on" duty, and carrying out of those activities, that takes us beyond normal human experience and wounds our souls so deeply.

Soldiers involved in dangerous circumstances...the ones who go beyond "every day" normal experiences...condition themselves subconsciously by adopting various coping methods. These are like firewalls installed on a computer to keep harmful data from entering and becoming destructive to the internal network.

While deployed these methods work well. They help maintain readiness, and at times, even help to maintain some sanity. When warriors engage in combat, it is easy for them to soon realize (or believe) that it is not a good idea to allow natural emotions to get loose while down range. If one did not shut down and allow a free-flowing of emotions, the risk of becoming useless to your mission and a liability to your comrades would become too great. "It don't mean nothin'..." in the opening of this chapter is a perfect example of that mindset.

As we wrote in our book, "Down Range: To Iraq and Back," troops in harm's way can ill afford to give way to emotions (of vulnerability, crying, grief, etc.) in the heat of battle, or when trying to accomplish a mission. These emotions must go on the back-burner, so to speak, and the deployed trooper learns to shut them down. It is this "shut down" mode that has caused so many negative issues upon returning to a civilian environment. A coping mechanism of this nature may be useful and necessary while engaged in a combat zone, but it is not a healthy reaction to bring back home. This kind of thinking is counterproductive when relating to those on the home front. Remember, they think differently than you do now about many aspects of life. Things have changed with you and with them. Now is the time to find some middle ground or neutrality in social interactions.

Finding *middle ground* is difficult due to many coping mechanisms instilled in warriors through training and wartime experiences. One of these is the numbing effect of "shut-down." What was once a useful coping method now becomes a hindrance in most civilian scenarios. To deal properly with this aspect of coping requires some re-thinking, skill-building through education—and a great deal of practice. Unfortunately, the military does not put much emphasis on re-training soldiers to be civilians...which makes a book like this a possible life-saver and necessary for surviving re-adjustment.

Reflection and Review

~Not talking about an experience does not make it disappear. Think of a few ways that silence (about your military duty) can be harmful to you and your relationships.

~"Firewalls" are natural defense systems that aid our survival in combat. In conventional situations, however, this shield or emotional barrier can put people and circumstances at a distance, causing detachment and a strain on relationships. Can you recognize the personal firewalls you now have as a result of your military duty? What do these firewalls look like? How are they affecting your present relationships?

CHAPTER TWO

MEETING
IN THE MIDDLE

"I am young, I am twenty years old; yet I know nothing of life but despair, death, fear .... What do they expect of us if a time ever comes when the war is over? Through the years our business has been killing; — it was our first calling in life. Our knowledge of life is limited to death. What will happen afterwards? And what shall come out of us?"
—Erich Maria Remarque "All Quiet on the Western Front"

Everyone has a specific job to do in the military. Like a team on the playing field, some block, some blitz, some receive, some score, etc., and a military unit is no different. Most do not have the job of negotiating with the enemy, and are not taught these skills. Going out into open territory with a white flag, or sitting down at a peace table has always been left to a few "experts," who generally know little about the struggles of soldiers engaged on a battlefield. The expert's job is to negotiate and talk with the enemy at a pre-ordained place that we call "middle ground."

Finding middle ground is better known as conflict resolution, and as soldiers we learn so little about this. Veterans have been challenged over the ages with the handicap of coming home and not being able to find peaceful and productive solutions to potentially volatile circumstances.

A couple of hours after hostile forces destroyed the World Trade Center on 9/11 this reality came home to me. I had watched the news reports and then gone to my scheduled focus group at the Veterans Administration. It was a quiet group that day, and like everyone else in America, every veteran in the group was confused and shocked. TV images of commercial jets crashing into skyscrapers, a smoldering Pentagon, and people leaping from flaming buildings swirled in our minds. All we could do was sit and stare at one another in disbelief.

Sitting silently for a long time we finally began to talk. I told them how I was feeling and about the sense of confusion I had. I told them, "Things like this happen and all I want to do is kill someone! I don't want to feel like this, but I don't have any tools to think differently. The Army never taught me how to deal with upsetting problems except by using combat tactics and now what do I do with the feelings I'm having? I'm not on active duty and can't do a thing about it…I guess I just don't know how to face and deal with stuff that ticks me off. I don't have a clue how to work it out, so where's the happy ending? It just seems to me like someone has to live and someone has to die—There's no in-between."

As I spoke, these words resonated with everyone in the room. Each veteran indicated he was personally struggling with similar thoughts. This made us realize as ex-combatants how little we knew about making peace with people when they trouble us so.

In my six years as a soldier, and two of them as a drill sergeant, I never once took a class about negotiating peaceful resolutions with anyone. No one instructed me in the area of compromise or problem solving. In war, conflict resolution focuses on closing with the enemy and eliminating him. When we could not overcome the enemy, we had only one response: retreat. We never got to a middle-ground agreement with them. Now as a civilian what does that look like? It could mean that when we get into an argument we become abusive, or on the other hand, we abandon the situation by walking out. We sometimes grope for settling things decently but have few or no tools to do so.

Attack, retreat, re-group, close ranks, don't bunch up, call in air support, etc. etc.; all of these military terms became the mantra by which we survived the most harrowing years of our lives. Without these principles, we faced death, defeat, pain, frustration, capture and a myriad of other less desirable outcomes. Only this mantra could bring us home alive.

Then it was back to civilian life and we carried on with this thinking because we were never instructed (or even reminded) on how to let go of our military modus operandi. As we re-enter conventional life and things get tough, we continue to resort to methods we know best—fight like hell or run the other direction. Neither are acceptable or healthy behavior on the home front.

It is easy to see that this pattern is destructive and severely impairs lasting relationships in a civilian world. In fact, these reactions, the defeat or retreat response, might be the reason why so many veterans have been charged with physical abuse and have been incarcerated over the years. For many, their only alternative (or method of conflict resolution) has been to fight. As they let loose of their pent up rage many lose control and physically hurt themselves or someone else. These responses become overused and can lead to a new level of regret.

For warriors desiring to get the most out of life after returning home from the war zone there is a great need to *re-train* (or re-think) and become conventional people again. As simple as that may seem, there are a couple of big obstacles that could hinder this process. Stress reactions, which are referred to as combat operational stress (COS), and/or post-traumatic stress disorder (PTSD), can make this transition and readjustment difficult. Attempting to re-enter civilian life with these major challenges makes it especially tough for most war veterans and their loved ones. One of these prevailing complications is what we refer to as the "wire syndrome."

Reflection and Review

~ Since peace talks are left up to only a few who are trained in negotiating with the opposition, the average warrior learns little about such skills. As the saying goes, "there is the right way, the wrong way, and the military way" of doing things. Learning proper methods of resolving conflicts for civilian encounters is generally *not* the military way. It is typical for veterans to either fight or flee in the face of adversity. This strong impulse to survive has been conditioned into them by their training.

Finding middle ground can best be described as neutralizing a situation by "coming to the table" where both parties will give and receive needed concessions to diffuse troubling issues. It is simply agreeing to extend the inner arms of grace to one another.

It is vital for you to understand how conflicts can be resolved in a positive way. Here are some ways to begin this process:

~ Do some personal inventory to identify and define the conflict. Who are the participants?

~ Now, create a list consisting of 5 or 6 possible outcomes that you would like to see transpire.

~Take responsibility for your actions and acknowledge your role, which is an important _____ factor leading to conflict resolution.

This requires an act of laying down your arms, which is not always easy for military personnel to do. Understand you are no longer in the war zone and having to deal with enemy fire.

~ Continue to do some personal discovery and find what works best for you to peacefully resolve issues with those around you.

CHAPTER THREE

WIRED FOR LIFE

"Before I deployed down range I was different around my wife and kids. Now that I'm back I can only let them get so close before I have to get away. I used to have fun letting my boys jump and crawl all over me. We would spend hours playing like that...Now I can only take a couple of minutes of this before I have to get out. I usually get in my truck and drive back to base to be with my platoon..."

The paratrooper who shared the above dilemma was part of a focus and support group we conducted while in Italy. Upon our invitation he and his comrades attended the meeting as part of the work we were doing with the 173d Airborne Brigade. They had recently re deployed from their combat tour in Northern Iraq.

The young sergeant was troubled with a family issue and came to the meeting seeking answers. He wanted to know why he now had such little tolerance for his two small children.

Their high energy had not bothered him before going off to war, but since returning, it had become too much for him. The way he found peace was to jump in his truck and drive back to the army base and spend time with some of his buddies with whom he had served in Iraq.

He went on to tell us how he was now afraid of the person he had become. His struggles with the change in his emotions and lower tolerance levels made him angry, and he was not holding things together as he once had. He said that while serving "down range" (engaged in a combat zone) he had complete control of his faculties almost all of the time. His cool capacity to endure, calculate, predict, and *tolerate* was spot-on and he was always "wired down tight." Now, two small children out of control with raucous play was sending him over the edge, and he felt like a failure. He did not understand how he could operate so effectively down range only to come home to lose it so easily with his kids.

The moment he told us he *had* to get away, and always felt better when he was back at the Army post with his buddies, Chuck caught on and had an idea what was going on. He then described some of his own similar reactions to life after he came home from Vietnam. When he told the sergeant about the "wire" he had strung up after Vietnam to keep others at a distance (and that he did not hug his three young sons for years because of this emotional defensive wall) the sergeant's face lit up.

To me it was a familiar expression. I have seen it many times in counseling sessions when veterans suddenly reach a point of new understanding and insight about the impact their military service has had on their lives. The relief they get from connecting the events in the war to the present situation is remarkable. They begin to see how these experiences now affect their present state of mind and those around them.

It was easy to see that the trooper was identifying with what another veteran was saying, and I could tell that the others in the group were learning something, too. The sergeant then began recalling times in Iraq when he subconsciously put into play the same emotional firewall that we were talking about earlier. He also saw how he had brought it home and kept it running like a computer with the files open. Chuck then asked if he had done this to protect his family from knowing the horrors of war he had lived through, and he nodded in agreement. I watched the entire group become aware and it seemed as if they were having their own defining moment as the discussion continued.

The "wire" was not a new reality for any of these men and women; but now that it had a definition, they could explain it to themselves because it finally had a *name* and a description.

In order to normalize the wire, I wanted to help them understand how this is a *normal* reaction to an abnormal set of circumstances. I clarified how in the heat of battle, or in the midst of a life-threatening experience, it is common to make reactive decisions and life-binding vows. Emotional subjects are avoided and not talked about; however, when they do come up, they are usually very deeply impacting moments for the warriors.

During times when men or women in uniform see people nearby hurt or killed, it is easy to decide that it may not be worth the emotional load (pain) to allow people to ever get close again. I went on to explain that if this wire, which is a defensive coping mechanism, remains buried and not outwardly processed, it becomes a liability. What they needed to hear most of all is that the "wire" they had put up was a normal reaction to the abnormal experiences they had endured. It was a way of protecting their hearts and those around them from the "baggage" they carried home from the war.

The sergeant smiled for the first time since arriving at the meeting and told us he needed to hear that. He finally realized that he was not alone in his feelings and it was normal for him to respond this way. I went on to encourage him that I knew how much he and his family would benefit by getting to know as much as possible about how this "perimeter" wire works.

As the meeting ended the atmosphere was much more relaxed than when it had started. Everyone got much out of it, and most importantly had learned about the wire. As for the sergeant, I'm hopeful that day was the beginning of a new dawn for his family, and that they have all found some wonderful healing moments together. To us, if he only went home and used a small portion of our discussion, we knew our work had been done. Likewise, the more that loved ones know about the wire, and why it exists, the easier it will be for them to accept the many different and peculiar ways that their warrior has changed.

The *wire* comes with the territory of war. It is all part of the experiences of combat that are imbedded in each warrior. Recognizing your own wire(s) and designing adaptive ways to cope will greatly enhance the effectiveness of the steps you need to take in coming home.

If you find yourself standing in open enemy territory and realize you are surrounded by mines, it is no time for a three-point sermon or a boring classroom lecture on the anatomy of explosive devices. You do exactly what you are trained to do and vacate the mine field in the most expeditious manner. It is time to step back, survey what is before you, and then deal with the wires you have in place. The first step out of this mine field is to find out how your wire works for and against you in conventional settings.

Reflection and Review

~ During times when we see people near us hurt or killed, it is easy to decide that it may not be worth the emotional pain to get close, or allow others to get close to us, ever again.

~ Can you recognize times in your past when you made decisions to create "self-defense" barriers in order to maintain distance between you and others for fear that you would get hurt emotionally?

CHAPTER FOUR

THE WORK OF A WIRE

"We forget nothing really. But so long as we have to stay here in the field, the front-line days, when they are past, sink down in us like a stone; they are too grievous for us to be able to reflect upon them at once. If we did that, we should have been destroyed long ago. I soon found out this much: terror can be endured so long as a man simply ducks; but it kills, if a man thinks about it."
—Erich Maria Remarque "All Quiet on the Western Front"

For many young people who become service members, the first time they have ever loved anyone beyond their immediate family is when they make friends (buddies) in training and in war. They become part of a close-knit military unit...and it is like a new family to them. They learn to love those with whom they entrust their lives. It is the witnessing of some of these close friends getting hurt that makes the pain so great, so they learn to avoid future pain by building their individual firewalls. The warriors exposed to such impacting events draw lines and string up perimeter wires to defend against future vulnerabilities.

The firewall computes and tells them that it is best not to get too close to anyone—so up goes the "wire" around us. It now exists to keep us from feeling any more pain because we "know" we have had enough to last us a lifetime.

When the war is over, there is a new twist to this phenomenon. Our subconscious firewalls do not go away by our just ceasing to fight. They remain in place, and as advanced as our military has become, there is little in place to help a warrior become a person who can once again think, react, and socialize as a civilian when enlistment is over. Veterans are virtually thrust back into a society that can now be difficult to relate to anymore.

Once back in the "real world" warriors are expected to be normal human beings again. As trained combatants we return firmly convinced that we will not allow anyone to cross over to certain points on our side of the wire. As a result we forfeit much intimacy and closeness with those who desire and expect it from us. Subconsciously we decide that if we did allow this crossing, and if anyone got hurt on "our watch," it would be too much to bear. As a result we maintain a wide "no-man's land" between us and the rest of the world, and so it begins—the emotional shut down, the separation, isolation and alienation.

So exactly what is the anatomy of the "wire?"

Sometimes, people find themselves in situations that can overwhelm them with helplessness, horror, and fear; it is especially impacting when they find themselves in danger of losing life and limb. These events are called traumatic experiences. Some common traumatic experiences can include physical attacks, being in serious accidents, serving in combat, sexual assaults, proximity to traumatic loss of life, or falling victim to fire or disaster such as a hurricane. These all can dictate to a person that a wire *must* go up in order to lessen the impact or prevent painful emotions. After traumatic experiences most people will likely find themselves having some problems that they did not have before the event.

Most combat veterans fully expect to return to normal life after war, but many seem to hit brick wall after brick wall when trying to allow others to get close for the intimacy they desire. The obstacle here is the *wire*, and it is one of the chief culprits that hangs people up in transitioning back to civilian life. It is, however, a method of self-protection not limited to only war veterans; when we describe "the wire," we find that people from all backgrounds express their familiarity with this mechanism. It is the duration of traumatic events for those who fight in a war that makes it so much more impacting.

The wire helps us maintain comfortable distances. It is a necessary means of keeping us from being hurt again. What is important to hear is that it was never strung up with the intention of *not* loving anyone or being loved. However, it does exist out of the secret fear that those near us could also get hurt if we "authorized" them to come too close.

After trauma this fear may dictate something like this: "If I let them come across to this side of the wire, and into my heart, I could never forgive myself if something happened to them. I'm not sure I could endure pain and anguish again like I had when my buddies got hit in the war." The next part of this mental computation is prompted by past trauma. It goes something like this: "It is better to keep them out, and even if it means that I am alone—I will be responsibly alone on this side of the wire, and I won't have the risk of losing again."

Summing it up, stringing up an emotional perimeter creates an invisible barrier used to keep others away. Sometimes this barrier is implemented through anger and aggressive tactics. So recognize this anger or emotion for what it is, and get to the core of why you are letting it cause more problems in your life. Remember, it is in place to deny others access to the emotional suffering and pain that is imbedded in a warrior's heart and mind. It is the inner person saying, "I've had enough! Don't come over because I don't want you to suffer with me."

We encourage you to identify your wire(s) and if you seriously take on this one simple project, it will do much in helping you make positive changes in your relationships and lifestyle.

The fully charged "juice" running through this wire electrifies the subconscious power of a perimeter line, and it is there to keep the rest of the world out.

Reflection and Review

~ Gaining awareness of your personal "wire(s)" is the first step in dealing with the negative ramifications it creates.

~ If you have recognized some of your wires, what do they look like, and how are they affecting your life?

CHAPTER FIVE

ADRENALINE...
JUICE IN THE WIRE

Troops do not make decisions as equals. Nor do they hear the reasoning behind the orders they receive. They just act on them. In turn, they are not conditioned to discuss feelings about decisions made by others who ordered them to carry out the acts of war. Considering alternatives to an order and circumventing orders for more comfortable options is not part of the program either. Military personnel receive orders and follow them. They simply obey and do not question.

What everyone (from the top of the chain of command to the bottom) counts on is for soldiers to perform tasks propelled by the hormonal "juice" called adrenaline. They rely on this juice to kick into action for the soldier to survive and overcome.

Military men and women often carry this method of conduct into their personal lives and into the process of transitioning back to civilian life. It is not uncommon for veterans who are parents to raise their children as though they were recruits in boot camp. I (Bridget) hear about it daily in my counseling practice from both vets themselves and their family members. It is difficult for loved ones to understand the order and discipline that is required while serving in a war zone.

Adrenaline is another aspect of the permanency of how the strain of war affects human biology. We hope you take this time to understand the concept of how adrenaline works for you—and against you. It is truly the fuel that drives many veterans from day to day. Consequently it has also caused many problems in their efforts going from soldier to civilian again. It works like this:

In our design and makeup, humans are geared for survival. The urge to survive is placed above all human instincts. In order to facilitate the impulse to live we have been equipped with two small glands located on the top of each kidney. These tiny glands are stimulated by our nervous system, and when we get upset or frightened, they secrete survival hormones. These chemicals pour into the bloodstream giving us new energy and strength to overcome the perceived danger. This sudden flow of hormones makes us stronger, and more alert. They protect us from blood loss, increase our lung capacity, sharpen our vision, and direct blood flow away from unnecessary organ functions to the large muscles of the body. These are known as adrenal glands.

When the adrenal glands are healthy, the reactions to danger are automatic and function completely at a subconscious level. Physiologists call this collection of physical changes the "fight or flight" response. They enable a frightened husband to lift the car off his injured wife; or they allow a terrified woman to run long distances for help. With this system fully functioning, our physical capacity for exceptional performance borders on the superhuman.

While this system keeps us alive in the face of extraordinary danger, it does have one major flaw. The reactive portion of the human brain cannot differentiate between a real threat and an imagined one! The brain does not notice or even care if it has encountered something real or a memory stimulated from something in the environment. Determined to keep us safe, it simply sends out the urgent signal to react. The adrenaline flows, and we function with automatic responses.

Adrenaline was designed to help us survive dangers, but to have it flowing from a *false alarm* can be dangerous to our own health. (It can also be unsafe for anyone close to us such as loved ones, friends, and people in general.) Not only does adrenaline put extra stress on critical body organs—like the heart and circulatory system—but the constant presence of adrenaline can be addictive—nearly addictive as an illegal drug. You have most likely heard the expression "that was a rush." This, of course, refers to the effects of our adrenaline surges.

In making the transition from a war zone...a life of constant alertness and danger...to one of relative calm, adrenaline rushes seem to work mostly against us. Once the "juice" surges, and the process begins, adrenaline is nearly impossible to control—especially after months of combat, where one's survival depends on adrenaline for prolonged periods of time. Our body becomes extremely efficient in starting and responding to the adrenaline response. What was meant to be a response for crisis becomes a way of life.

In human relationships in civilian life, the adrenaline cycle can send us down two equally destructive pathways. Combat veterans suddenly diving for cover when a car backfires or fireworks explode are a good case in point. The noise signals danger; their brain, unable to differentiate between a real or imagined threat, begins the adrenaline cycle. An old imprinted message

ONCE A WARRIOR

tells them to move into action and survive. Without thinking, they respond just as they did in the war zone. Most of the time, their response is inappropriate for peacetime situations.

The "trigger" (something in the immediate environment that is a *reminder*) can be a sight, smell, sound, or any combination of numerous other sensory perceptions that may be associated with a past threat or injury. When these sudden triggers occur, the veteran may suffer tremendous emotional upset. Many repressed emotions come flooding back without much warning. Feelings associated with wartime experiences, such as fear, pain, anger, helplessness, and confusion can surface almost immediately.

When this cycle happens in the presence of those close to the veteran, they, too, are affected by the behavior. They may feel frustrated because they do not understand or cannot help. This kind of scenario most likely will embarrass the unsuspecting veteran and to protect oneself and those nearby, the warrior may even attempt to put more distance between them.

As warriors consider their triggers they may generalize their experiences or refuse to talk about them, which is another way of avoiding future re-stimulation. Their emotional withdrawal and physical isolation creates confusion in loved ones, and this destructive pattern further diminishes the chance of sustaining healthy relationships.

Sudden flowing adrenaline can produce a kind of hormonally induced "high." When trauma survivors, and especially combat veterans, constantly experience this adrenaline flow in the presence of conflict—a response that was perfectly acceptable in a time of danger or the heat of battle—the resulting "high" they experience becomes rewarding in itself. In order to feel this *high* it is not uncommon for situations to be "manufactured" to create the need for the adrenaline rush.

This high, the rage generated by conflict, can become a pattern, burned into the brain like a computer burns a CD. It can become as rewarding as the high of drugs or alcohol. Rage can lead to irrational behavior or acts of violence expressed against anyone—even loved ones. This hormonally induced behavior can stimulate the kind of violence that puts many veterans in jail.

Anger has no place in conflict resolution in a civilian world. When it erupts into rage, it stimulates the kind of "fight or flight" cycle that is common with people who are charged up with adrenaline. This escalates the hormonal response of the body. The hormones in turn stimulate more rage, and the body prepares for action. Our ability to listen, to reason, and to communicate logically diminishes; and a veteran's worst fear, *being out of control,* occurs.

In the following *Reflection and Review* we offer you some tools to learn more about short-circuiting the process of adrenaline over-dose.

Reflection and Review

~ Self-control is a valuable asset for us all. Here are some suggestions on how to control overdoses of adrenaline:

~ Do a "body scan." Ask yourself, *where do I feel that shot of adrenaline most in this situation?* Pay attention to your body as you experience the first feelings of anger or uptightness. Do your jaw muscles tighten? Do your hands grow cold? Does your breath come in little puffs? Associate those physical sensations with your increasing tension, and use them as a signal to take a break. Do not be afraid to say, "I need to take a walk right now. Can we discuss this later?" This is not a sign of weakness, and is perfectly acceptable, whether you are talking with the boss, your wife, or a customer relations person from a large company on the phone.

~ Do not let your anger build to the point that it feeds the adrenaline cycle. If you are with a stranger, take yourself away physically. Leave the room. Get off the freeway. Hang up the phone. Do whatever you need to do to remove yourself from the trigger (stimulus) *before* the cycle begins to spin out of control.

~ After you withdraw do what you can to relax. Take deep breaths. Take your mind off the conflict and try to think or do something positive. Create a positive distraction to focus on—one that will calm you down. You may need to lean against a wall just to ground yourself into the present. Consider exercise as a means to burn off accumulating adrenaline. Take a walk or go for a run. Know what your body needs before heading out on the multiple journeys the day can bring for you. Only when you are back in control should you try again to solve that issue. The longer you go between cycles of symptomatic triggering, the less power the out-of-control adrenaline holds over you.

CHAPTER SIX

STANDING DOWN: A CLASH IN REALITIES

It is over. You have done what few people have done, or will ever do in their lifetime...you have gone to war and survived.

As the time to re-enter civilian life approaches many changes hang on the horizon. The closer that time comes the more critical it is to identify and familiarize yourself with some of the modifications you will need to effectively make a transition. When the discipline and regulations of being in the military wind down, there can be a sense of trepidation about being thrust back into a world where standards and expectations are not what you have become accustomed to.

Before entering the service your life was different. What you now have become familiar with, and is now second-nature as a soldier, may cause you to wonder how (or if) your unique military experiences will ever fit into a civilian life. Few civilian jobs, or situations, call for such a high focus on national security, personal discipline, and combat tactics that you lived with day in and day out while in uniform. (Fortunately in today's military many of the specialties do translate well to the civilian job market, but this does not alleviate many of the unique transitional issues.)

One of the first realizations I (Chuck) had upon entering civilian life after six years in the U.S. Army, and one in a war zone, was: Civilians are dangerous people! Most have no idea how close to the path of harm's way they trod. They seem oblivious to the danger many of their actions, attitudes, and habits are capable of causing. A soldier learns and knows pretty much all the time what he or she is capable of. Along with that, the prevalence of, and the handling of, lethal weapons are commonplace in the military while few jobs in the civilian world require or allow this. Within our training we become used to going on tactical alert at any time to handle situations. We do this by executing the maximum amount of power in our possession to accomplish a mission, keep people safe, and eliminate threats...all at the same time.

The headline news for me was that these "trained-in" instincts do not work well when interacting as a civilian. In 1967, upon realizing how much I had changed due to my training and experiences, the only solution I had was to re-enlist for another hitch. I did this to keep myself out of trouble with the law and/or so I would not hurt someone and find myself locked up. The only safe harbor I could think of was to be back in uniform and within the secure confines of a military environment. However, when it comes to transitional options, staying in the service may not be a plan of your choice. This is one very good reason why we have written this book.

My (Chuck) next discovery, since I process information orally, was that I needed to talk to someone about where I had been and what I had done in Vietnam. It was extremely difficult to explain war experiences to civilians. They just did not fully grasp certain things like chains of command, shoot-move-communicate, and most other aspects of military life. It all became so frustrating that I decided it was best to just shut up. I know this has also become a major source of irritation for many ex-warriors over the years. However, this is equally exasperating for loved ones who are being shut out because they no longer view the world as you do.

Verbalizing the details of traumatic events is tough to do for those who have been to war. Attempting to explain the context, including the reasons for decisions that led up to the traumatic event, and the tremendous sense of urgency that prevails when under fire, has always been challenging for veterans. Almost like a sixth sense, they feel that those who have never been there will not get the full gist of their experience. It is no surprise that since Vietnam, veteran-to-veteran focus groups have been quite effective in helping vets sort through some of these troubling issues. One of the reasons it is effective is because the veterans find an opportunity to share with those to whom they can relate and identify. This in itself has terrific healing power.

Often our troops return to hometowns that are far from a base or fellow military personnel. Thus, the luxury of speaking with healthy and positively motivated veterans is not always easy to find. Your local veteran's center, or veteran's hospital, is an excellent way to connect with other veterans and there are many resources available to you. Speaking with a highly trained and caring civilian, who is knowledgeable of the military life, can be highly beneficial as well. It is advisable not to do this alone; dealing with your post traumatic stress requires teamwork and your pro-active approach in making the connections. The willingness to work through the recovery process is entirely up to you.

Reflection and Review

~How well do you handle stress?

The daily stress in civilian life is usually more trivial than traumatic. How you cope with lesser problems than you became accustomed to in the war zone — such as a disgruntled boss at work, or your Internet going on the blink — can reveal much about your potential reaction to more serious setbacks. Here is a simple test to see how well you are doing:

1. You are called in for a second interview and this could be the job of a lifetime. What do you choose to do first to prepare?

A] I'll close myself in and tune everything out so I can focus on the interview.
B] I'll put on my IPod, listen to some sounds, and take a walk to calm myself.
C] I'll add this to a long list of other things I am currently juggling.

2. Your family has expressed some disappointment that you are not the same as you were when you left for the war. How do you react?

A] I'll do whatever they want—I just want to make everyone happy.
B] I realize I cannot satisfy everyone—all the time. I am at peace with that.

C] I'll prepare a statement to give them so they understand. Perhaps this will get them off my back.

3. Your job and work has become therapeutic for you but others see it as your hang-up since coming home from the war. Where are you on this?

A] Those around you get little of your time and attention because you are "all work and no play".
B] When I am off the clock, I'm off the clock. Work does not spill over to my personal life.
C] I am working to make my family's lifestyle better, and even if they don't understand why I work all the time now, they will appreciate my efforts some day.

Answer key:
1. A = 2   B = 1   C = 3
2. A = 2   B = 1   C = 3
3. A = 3   B = 1   C = 2

Score your reactions. The higher the score the lower your threshold is for allowing PTSD and COS to affect your life:

3 – 6 = You are handling pressing problems just as you should.
6 – 9 = You are susceptible to extreme levels of stress (PTSD or COS).

CHAPTER SEVEN

HAPPY TO BE HOME...
BUT I MISS THE ACTION

"As strange as it seems, inside there's a need to get back to the war. I can't tell my folks this because they'll think I'm not glad to be home. I feel trapped, and like someone who is schizo or something. I'm glad to be back, but there's something always gnawing at me and I can't figure it out...I feel really confused."
—An OIF Veteran

Up to this point in this book we have gone over many details about war stress. It was important to do this in order to lay the ground work for understanding why some veterans struggle after coming home from a war zone. As we move on we will cover some other ground level issues that can be troublesome in getting back to conventional life once military duty is over.

Through the years of counseling veterans it is amazing how many I (Bridget) have known to live on the edge via risky pastimes, hobbies, or habits. Much of this has to do with the subject of adrenaline, which we discussed in detail earlier; but there is another reason for this as well.

Countless times I have heard veterans, especially the younger veterans of the present (OIF/OEF) war, tell me how disappointed they are with civilian life. Most miss being with their buddies in the war zone and have an unsettled longing to be with them again. Many unsettled vets find ways to cope by coming to roost with "happy" mediums such as riding fast motorcycles, skydiving, or going off crab fishing in the cold and treacherous waters of Alaska. High energy and high risk activities keep them busy with little time to think about the war. It is, of course, a way to *avoid* the deep issues stewing inside as well. Along with the avoidance it provides them with the "fix" they need to maintain a high adrenaline level in order to feel alive and at the top their game. The high keeps them from fixating on the boredom that civilian life has become.

Others do not find that place of satisfaction so easily and spend many hours in my office trying to come to terms with why they are so edgy, uptight, and angry... "all for no good reason." They admit to being disappointed because civilian life has not rematerialized as they thought it would when they got out. Home versus war zone becomes an inner conflict. On one hand they are happy to be safely home and removed from the miseries of life "down range;" but on the other they cannot bear it because home is too complicated. Things were much simpler when they were in the war zone. They always knew what they were going to wear, what the daily schedule was, and what was expected of them.

As reality sets in, the other factor weighs heavily; it was not just the war they left behind. It was their brothers and sisters-in-arms. They also left people who had become, in many ways, closer than blood kin through the tests of "fire." There are no other relationships in this world so strongly welded together as those they formed and left behind in the war zone. When they stepped onto that plane and came home, they walked away from comrades whose lives depended on them while down range. Conversely, they, too, put their own lives in the hands of those friends on a daily basis. Many admit they feel guilty about now living a life of ease here in the States while those same friends are still in harm's way. On one level it is almost as if they cannot allow themselves to be happy knowing that their military family is still down range—and at risk.

One recent report talks of a 32-year old female soldier, and mother of four small children, who has been home from Iraq for several months. She still calls her unit every day to check on her buddies, and yet she has not spent any time with her children since being home. They live with relatives while she tries to unravel her life as a soldier. She has not decided where she really fits in; and the expectations of returning from the war zone to a family, with psychological issues, can be overwhelming.

I (Chuck) remember my reactions to the 20th anniversary of the fall of Saigon. It was aired over and over on most news networks, and I had some very mixed emotions. We 'Nam vets have been told so many times that we "lost" the war when, in fact, we feel the politicians just quit on us and we veterans were stuck with a lot of undue blame for a lie. To have such fanfare over the finality to that war caused too many bad reminders for most of us, and it was tough to bear.

One of the prevailing feelings I had at the time was that we were not able to finish the job in Southeast Asia. Over the years I have had other veterans tell me the same thing…many of whom are Korean War veterans. Now I hear the same from OIF/OEF troops, and at the time of this writing their war is not even over yet.

A job left undone these days for veterans has much to do with the all-volunteer military. These young men and women consider themselves to be professionals and they enlisted to be trained in a professional manner. When they accept the option of returning to civilian life (while the war is continuing), they leave military jobs that they did well and were proud of doing only to return to a life that is now different and filled with anxiety.

With modern media, Internet, and other forms of communication, average Americans are exposed more than ever to real-time news. OIF/OEF veterans now at home are bombarded with live news directly from the combat zone(s). It is difficult for these men and women not to feel that they are somehow still responsible for pulling their share of the load, and it is especially difficult when they find out that it was their unit that got hit and took casualties that day. They feel that if they had been there with them, perhaps they could have done something differently, and the outcome would not have been so grave. In reality, it is probable that there was little they could have done to change the course of events from tragedy to triumph.

Reflection and Review

~ Take a break from the news. When you watch television or listen to radio, tune to the stations that are uplifting and emotionally "nutritious" in order to enhance your more positive interests.

~ Do an inventory of your daily and weekly activities and determine if they are helping you side-step some issues that, if dealt with, could improve your life. High energy activities may keep you busy with little time to think about the war, but sometimes we need to stop and ask ourselves, "Is this a way to *avoid* some things I should be facing?"

CHAPTER EIGHT

A FRAME OF MIND

IS IT TIME TO RE-BOOT...
OR CUT AND PASTE?

The subject of re-behaving coined by Bill Cosby, which fits so well in describing the transition process from soldier to civilian, has much to do with viewing and inspecting old pictures. These are the mental images stored away in your mind that came home with you. They are the ones that were imbedded during military service, and which will affect most of your civilian decisions, reactions, and activities for years to come.

"Un-doing" or "re-framing" these pictures are significant keys to a happier more fulfilling life in the world. It is important to either *un-do* or *re-frame* your training so you can find ways to make good returns/transitions into the life you have looked forward to. In other words, examine your military occupational specialty (MOS) and determine how the responsibilities you had in the military now translate to the civilian job market.

It takes some skill for both *un-doing* and *re-framing*. We hope we can help you attain some of these skills. Re-frame for example can mean to take a military function and convert it into *proficiencies* so that it will enhance your civilian work or behavior. This is much like we have done in later sections in this book.

Un-doing, on the other hand, is the process of finding ways to *extricate* ourselves from activities, responses, and attitudes and beliefs that do not translate into productive civilian behaviors, or habits.

(A note of advice: If what has been "trained-in" persists, and proves to be a detriment, you may consider seeking professional help; and we emphasize that doing so does not in any way indicate a sign of weakness! We want to commend you for seeking support and direction to enhance this part of your readjusting to civilian life.)

After close assessment of how your life is working or not working, it may be time to take on a new perspective, and see life from a new set of eyes. This is the new view of a person who has been transformed by his or her experiences in the war zone. If you continue to see that something is not working, or your relatives and close friends are commenting on how you have changed, this may be a sign that what they *see* should be taken to heart. As painful as it is sometimes to admit, from time to time we need to take inventory, and now may be the time to make that move.

Re-framing involves taking a situation and analyzing it from various angles to get a true reading on what is happening. You conduct your own inspection. At that point you take what you see and change so it fits into the lifestyle or situation that you are attempting to develop and enhance.

For example, a soldier recently said to me, "Bridge, I've had it! Everywhere I go people just move so slow—they seem to always mope along. Whether it's on the highway, or a line at the store, I always seem to get stuck behind them. I feel like I'm ready to explode from frustration." My response was, "Have you ever stopped to think that there is a reason why you are held up, and why you seem to be left to deal with this frustration? I see these times as opportunities for you to learn how to relax. Perhaps you need to recognize that most things are out of your control anyway, and the more you try to control them the worse they become. It could be that these situations come across your path as a means of helping you step back, slow down, and take a deep breath so you can work on being more patient."

Later I received an email from him. He said that what I had shared on re-framing with him was one of the most helpful things he had ever been told. He went on to tell me how much it had changed his perspective. By re-framing those moments of frustration he was beginning to turn them into opportunities to slow down and smell the roses more than ever.

Re-framing is sort of like cutting and pasting on our computer. Sometimes we are like a computer that gets overloaded with data, and when stress is a factor, it sometimes does not take much to go over the edge (or crash). When one is conditioned and trained in the military, these values, skills, etc. are stored deep in the subconscious; they become second nature. It is a matter of survival and has become a trained-in stimulus response pattern when faced with life or death decisions.

However, it becomes important to override this conditioning when you return to the civilian world. Many of these patterns will end up costing you and your family dearly if you do something regretful. So, it is time to re-boot and run a new program, one that will be much more conducive to transitioning from warrior to civilian in a positive way.

How Survival Surveillance Works Against Us:

While on duty in the military, extreme surveillance is practiced and drilled over and over again. Being alert is what keeps one alive and successful as a warrior; however, this is one combat attribute that needs an "about face" when re-entering civilian life. The same levels of threats are not prevalent in most conventional situations, but since warriors are geared by their training to keep their "radar" up, their reaction mode does not fit well back on the home front. With post-traumatic stress and combat occupational stress the volume level of our environment is turned up too loud, and "survival surveillance" is a conditioned routine that intensifies when we try to tune to our surroundings. What we want to do is help you turn the volume down.

It is proper and good judgment to be aware of danger, but the problem with "survival surveillance" is that the fight or flight, live-or-die thinking, creates anxiety and anxiety gives birth to many inappropriate false alarms. These false alarms are what make us feel (or seem to others to be) unstable and volatile. It is this intense survival mechanism that needs to be leveled out in order to make good transitions.

To begin with, overriding your system by adapting and using new coping methods will help you begin to interfere with the subconscious conditioning process that the military has installed on your hard drive. Combat survival modes are programs now running on automatic and are stored in the subconscious mind. The simplest method of coping with (override) this is to remain in the present, and refuse to allow yourself to visit places in your mind that will trigger old videos (memories); by doing so you will be able to by-pass that which has been instilled deep inside you.

A FRAME OF MIND

One of the most effective ways to remain in the here-and-now is to practice the art of "locating" yourself. What I mean by this is when you feel as if you are going out of sorts, begin to look at your environment and identify where you are NOW. What are your immediate surroundings? (One bit of advice is to ask your family or close friends who spend time with you to also help you out.) If you need to, physically walk up to something near you and touch it. Identify what it is (it could be anything…a wall, a telephone pole, your car, etc.) and say the name of what you are feeling. You could even describe the texture, temperature, etc. Sometimes just looking at the landscape and verbally explaining what you see will help you return to the present. If someone is nearby perhaps he or she can help ground you by changing the topic or asking you questions about something unrelated to your trauma. Maybe that person can also help you get into the present by drawing your attention to your immediate, present-time surroundings. It is amazing how this simple little technique will draw you to the present, and away from a tendency to be on high alert and out-of-sorts with your immediate environment. In reality, by consciously "locating" (or grounding) yourself is to *override* what you have been trained to do.

This is one more step in learning to "re-behave" It will help you to manage enough to by-pass the systems that kept you alive in the combat zone — systems that are not appropriate for your conventional life back home.

As an extension of these thoughts, in making the leap from soldier to civilian it is important to learn some skills in recognizing how the imbedded viewpoints you now use may affect your life. In the next few chapters we address these skills and how they translate to your life on the home front.

Reflection and Review

~ For warriors to "re-frame" means to convert a military skill into a conventional proficiency so that it will enhance your civilian work or behavior. "Un-doing," on the other hand, is the process of finding ways to extract ourselves from activities, responses, and attitudes that do not translate into productive civilian behaviors or habits.

~ Do an inventory of your skills and experiences. Now determine if you must re-frame or un-do these in order to successfully make a transition into the civilian workplace and social environment. Ask yourself: *Have my viewpoints and behaviors been problematic in the civilian world?* If so, how must you go about re-framing and un-doing these ways?

CHAPTER NINE

A JOB LOST IN TRANSLATION

You just know you are ready to hit the streets. Now with your experiences and all the heavy stuff behind you, civilian life is going to be a piece of cake. You are a survivor! Let it begin!!!

This is true. However, it is a good idea to pick a point of entry and start this journey back to civilian life in the driver's seat. It is sort of like when you got into a Humvee for a patrol, supply delivery, or any other reason to go outside the wire and be on the roads down range. You prepared and would never just haphazardly climb in and go without any thought given as to what you would need just to accomplish your objective—or have a way out if you ran into trouble.

As innocent and peaceful the social environment back in the States seems, you may discover some surprises along the way. It might not be comfortable for you when you see yourself respond or perceive the challenges involved. We encourage you to stay alert and do what you can to mentally prepare for these unexpected twists and turns. We hope to help you do this, and the workplace is a good place to begin because going back to school or getting a job are usually the top priorities, and goals such as these give you purpose and focus.

Many times after getting released from active duty the major challenge is to figure out what you can do to move forward with your life. Fortunately in today's military the professionalism and job specialization has made a great deal of advancement in educating personnel. Our troops are getting more technical skills even with a war going on. We meet young veterans all the time who are working in jobs that have been secured due to their military schooling and experience. It is safe to say that skills, qualifications, and competency levels are increased for our veterans when they separate from the military. Today's troops are trained in doing a large variety of jobs and this is not a major issue for them. They are generally well-trained and adept in many areas suited for today's job market. To a large degree our ex-military personnel are an untapped, and sometimes under-utilized, resource in today's work force in America.

It is the stressful experiences while performing those jobs when deployed that continue to be roadblocks and problems for those who return from the war zones. It behooves us to look for every possible avenue in helping you find ways to successfully adapt to conventional life once again. When warriors return home, all the training in the world will not eradicate the memories, suffering, and myriad of other psychological issues they face. These are issues we cannot ignore and we will continue to have a need to confront them head-on as we go along. However, as in the past—and as it will be in the future of warfare—there are *some* occupational skills that have proven to be difficult in their translation to the civilian arena.

For an infantryman and for those in other direct combat related specialties, shoot, move, and communicate is what combatants live by and what keeps them alive in war. If these procedures are primarily what you experienced down range, then new snags will form in the transition net of warrior to civilian.

A combat-ready mindset is to maintain the inner resolve and strength to face fear, obstacles, and trials in battle with courage and coolness of character. Assaulting and retreating, with little or no opportunity to negotiate with the opposition, is not how civilians normally resolve issues. Even police work, which is a closely-related job skill to a combat MOS (military occupational specialty), focuses primarily on peaceful resolutions and safety. Eliminating enemy forces or bad elements is a last resort in most cases; however, for those who have returned home from the war zone this component still rings strong and adds more frustration to an already edgy combatant.

I (Chuck) once attended a veterans' employment symposium. After a few hours of encouraging lectures and presentations we (veterans) were invited to look through several large reams of papers for a job that would fit for us. Supposedly these huge stacks of copied and bound books contained civilian jobs that could be paralleled and matched with the MOS in which we were trained while on duty.

Most of the military specialties listed had a good amount of civilian jobs matching them; for example, an administrative clerk literally had thousands of possible civilian counterparts that a trained person could consider pursuing. My MOS upon on being released from the military was 11B...infantry rifleman. I had been trained to take care of my feet while on long marches, and learned how to ensure all the gear on my back was strapped on properly so it did not make noise while on patrol in enemy territory. I knew how to keep a weapon clean in wet and dirty conditions, and I could use it effectively to defend or aggress against opposing forces. Matching jobs? Maybe I could be a policeman, a correctional officer, or perhaps even a park ranger if I could get myself through enough of the years of college that were needed. This was pretty doubtful, since the political climate on college campuses would have created too many problems for me to deal with at the time. As much as I looked through those stacks of papers I found few, or no, civilian jobs that matched what I had trained for and done while in the service.

Since I could fall back on some job experience before entering the service, I was able to find some decent work. Those years spent in the military however, were of little use to me when it came down to finding *relative* gainful employment. I was constantly challenged to find creative ways to make a decent living. During the time when other young people trained at tech schools or were educated in universities, I was soldiering…doing soldier things. I lost those years that could have been spent advancing my employment worth.

Many young people who have entered our present volunteer military never joined to fight a war. Most enlisted to get educational benefits and job skills that would enhance their lives once they become civilians again. It (the war) just happened along the way as history seems to repeat itself, and these bright young Americans have been caught in the middle. Consequently, they have been asked to make national defense and military matters a priority.

America Can Help

It is our hope that America reads this book as well as all warriors and their families — especially those in positions to forward the lives of those returning from war zones and focused on re-entering the civilian employment arena.

There are many organizations that have dedicated them-selves to this task. One particular organization geared to help employers and veterans connect is One-Stop Career Centers. It is a federal government program. The HireVetsFirst website (www.HireVetsFirst.gov) will direct you to more than 2,000 of these centers nationwide. Other websites that help both veteran and employer connect are www.usajobs.gov, and www.ajb.org. At USAJOBS you can create and post job listings for positions with the Federal Government as well as search for veterans who are looking for employment. America's Job Bank (AJB) is a component of the One-Stop Career Center network. Here you can post listings, create customized job orders and search resumes to find highly trained veterans with all types of skills.

As for resume work, many Goodwill organizations around the country have free training in resume writing for veterans. It is a branch of Goodwill Vocational Services. There are also websites available that will help you write a proper resume.

Fortunately, for the nation's sake and for our safety, some of those who are educated and trained while in the service also decide to make careers in the military.

Reflection and Review

~ If your military occupational specialty is difficult to translate to the civilian workplace, take advantage of the educational programs that are available for veterans. However, the training in today's military for all occupational specialties should give you an edge in choosing a desirable field of work. There are many organizations that give veterans special consideration in employment matters; *always* mention that you are a veteran when inquiring.

CHAPTER TEN

PROVEN STRENGTHS

Every individual has his or her own way of making the journey from war to peace. One commonality of all who transition back into civilian life from the military is that they have much to bring to the table. They can consider their time spent and the training they received as an investment and a valuable resource, and now it is time to cash in and receive some profits. A *good return* coping action is to convert your combat skills so they work for you in a civilian world. This allows you to capitalize on those things you now know and possess. These attributes have already proven to be valuable strengths in your personal arsenal.

Personal Strengths by Serving in the Military:

It is always good to step outside and look back in when trying to learn something about yourself. The first part of our transitional process is to do just that. We will move you outside to have a look. You can then do an exterior inspection of your interior. You will be able to objectively see what is inside; i.e., where you have been, what you have learned, and done during your military life. The process is much like doing an inventory of your personal equipment. First you identify, then tally up, and finally codify all you have in order to evaluate and determine your assets and liabilities.

Let's begin by listing some of the strengths you attained during your military experience and then parallel these to some benefits in civilian life.

Military strength:

Camaraderie — unit cohesion and teamwork.

Ask any soldier and he or she will tell you that one of the most precious features to military life is the bond made with whom they serve. The teamwork welded together many times in order to survive life and death situations cannot be topped by many other experiences in a lifetime. For many young people it is their first crack at living in a relational "community" where personal survival depends on buddies, and vice versa. These bonds are intense and loyal.

Strength matched to civilian life:

Friendships and Teamwork — relationship support systems. This asset promotes and inspires the strength that lies within the concept of unity. Team builders, connection specialists (i.c. consultants and matchmakers), and personnel organizers are highly sought after in business, building relationships, family, civic activities, work, and team careers. You know how to get along with various types of people in stressful situations. This is a great talent developed through some hard times. Use it well.

Military strength:

Tactical alertness — vigilant and watchful.
You have been fine tuned to be on constant "guard duty." As any combat-ready and experienced soldier can attest, to know the potential dangers on a road, trail, or line of march is essential when in the field. To see the enemy before he sees you is vital to safely accomplish a mission. When you are securing and protecting equipment, information and personnel on bases, you are also a major target for attack. Alertness and the utmost vigilance is mandatory in order to stay alive.

Strength matched to civilian life:

Peripheral mental vision — administrative preparedness.
The instilled alertness you now possess can be converted and utilized to foresee and identify situations and signs of potential trouble to self, family, groups, and work. Just as on a military operation, the element of surprise is key in determining many outcomes; you need to turn that around. Your training has reinforced a wonderful sense of predictability and you will

not be easily surprised as often as those around you. You can anticipate what others may not be able to see. Use it to your advantage to do well and advance yourself.

Military strength:

Armed for combat — constant close proximity to lethal weapons and maintained safety.

Weapon safety is the backbone of all basic combat training. Military personnel learn to live eat, sleep, drink and think *with* their weapons and live ammunition. To those with a combat MOS, loaded weapons become an extension of their body and most feel naked without one on their person. In that training, however, every soldier learns first and foremost the importance of safety and is penalized heavily for any carelessness. Within the concept of being aware of the destructive capabilities of these weapons comes a unique level of awareness attained by every trained military person—regardless of military occupational specialty. It is a special attentiveness to the danger contained within their controlled sphere of influence, and the instilled steps of caution they automatically take to use that power in a way that minimizes risk to oneself and those with whom they serve.

Strength matched to civilian life:

Creation of safe environments — Protector.

This training has given you the ability to establish creative preventive measures against possible threats of your person and loved ones. It has also given you a special sense of paying attention to situations to which civilians for the most part may be oblivious. This awareness of harmful or destructive possibilities in your surroundings can enhance the *predictabil-*

ity level mentioned above. This is an asset that you can transition easily into your civilian occupation, social life and/or family environments.

Military strength:

Emotional control under pressure — not easily rattled and in control.

In your training and wartime experiences you found there was little time, or place, for a release of most emotions that are inherent in human beings. To effectively accomplish a mission one cannot break down emotionally. During an exercise, or actual combat, natural coping occurs which shuts down emotions that you know will be a liability to your safety, your teammates, and the mission.

Strength matched to civilian life:

A calm, cool, collected person — a rare asset.

Being on top of things while under pressure is a wonderful asset. When others are out of control, you have a built-in ability to stay calm and effectively handle situations. It is this calm strength by which people determine and make selections in such areas as employment, romance, social endeavors, etc. You have a quality that relatively few civilians ever exercise or possess. Put it into action.

Military strength:

Disciplined and commanding presence — can take charge and lead when others cannot.

Every warrior is trained to step up and take charge during demanding times. The chain of command instills this in every soldier. When, and if, they become the ranking person, the position of authority is automatically assumed. By operating and living in an environment where leadership is always acknowledged, respected, and followed, military personnel are accustomed to that order, and are always prepared to take their share of responsibility in getting missions effectively completed.

Strength matched to civilian life:

First impressions are not easily forgotten — an image of confident assurance.

As in any military unit, when presenting yourself in civilian circumstances, how you initially come across to others determines many outcomes. In everyday military life you were called upon to present yourself as orderly, prepared, and knowledgeable of your duties and affairs. Routine inspections drilled you in this feature of military life. With this training you acquired a skill to be able to present yourself in similar ways to employers and others to whom personal advancement would depend. Few civilians are ever taught how to prepare (clothes, personal grooming, etc.) for such presentations.

Reflection and Review

~ Review some of the training that was central in leading you to where you presently are. Once you look it over it is essential to determine any *corresponding* activities and mindsets that the civilian world has to offer and then pursue them.

~ Review some of the effective and compatible tools mentioned in this chapter that make productive use of your military competency. You are an untapped resource.

CHAPTER ELEVEN

TRIPWIRES ON THE OBSTACLE COURSE

If you remember, the training obstacle course prepared you to move over, under, and around those things that would impede maneuverability during combat. Likewise, there are some specific obstacles or hurdles to cross when beginning the transition from warrior to civilian.

To further help you recognize some of these transitional difficulties we have listed some important comparisons for you to use and become aware of. They are the three "R's"...*recognize, renew and redefine.*

The following measurements illustrate the differences between your military duty and conventional life at home. Your lifestyle, actions, and reactions while in the war zone contained many positive aspects; however, you will see that these may now have some adverse consequences if used inappropriately in a civilian environment.

They are:

1. Camaraderie — unit cohesion and teamwork

The Front = Your life was entrusted to your buddies, and no one else understands your experience but those with whom you served.

Home Front hurdle:

The Home Front = You may long and prefer to be with your war buddies rather than with your loved ones. Your understanding and interests are elsewhere. You avoid talking because everything seems unimportant compared to what you have been through. You may come across as "cold" and "aloof" to loved ones and others.

Recognize, renew, and redefine:

The Home Front = Recognize and utilize your training skills to renew family ties. Spend individual time with loved ones. Accept and provide support. Recognize that everyone has changed and now it is time to redefine yourself and what you have become in the time of your absence.

2. Tactical alertness — vigilant and watchful

The Front = Survival depends on constant awareness of surroundings and reacting to danger according to your training (sniper fire, mortar attacks, possible IEDs, etc.)

Home front hurdle:

The Home Front = Inappropriate triggers set you off. You are hyper-vigilant and anxious in crowds and small confined spaces. You become easily startled and have difficulty with sleep because you must be on guard.

Recognize, renew, and redefine:

Train yourself to recognize and anticipate what is a *minor* or *major* event or a change in your surroundings. Familiarize yourself with the elements in your environment that repeatedly set off combat-induced triggers. Once you familiarize yourself with this information, use it to avoid being over-reactive.

Implement an exercise program. Refrain from large amounts of alcohol or illegal (street) drugs to help with sleep.

3. Armed for combat — constant close proximity to lethal weapons

The Front = Mandatory possession of weapons. You were required to carry a weapon for the purpose of dealing with conflict, aggression and personal protection. You have it ready for action all the time. It meant life or death.

Home front hurdle:

The Home Front = You travel nowhere outside the home without being armed. (Remember a family picnic is no place for a weapon.) The feeling of being "naked" without a weapon (firearm, or knife) in your possession can become a prevailing issue, inducing fear and anxiety among those in your presence. Carrying dangerous, and sometimes illegal, weapons in cars and on your person everywhere you go is not using good judgment. Many times war veterans have a compulsive belief that loved ones are never safe unless they are armed.

Recognize, renew, and redefine:

Align combat laws with civilian laws. Combat law dictates – You have skills that were developed and practiced down range. You know the strict rules for weapon safety, and you know where and/or when to fire a weapon. Civilian law dictates safety precautions. Never drive with a loaded weapon, or use a weapon to threaten or intimidate others (especially those close to you…especially loved ones). Do not demand anything from anyone by brandishing a weapon. Do what you can to wean yourself from the security of carrying dangerous firearms.

As a note of interest: We, the authors are not advocating for gun control, or any changes in any of the Constitutional Amendments regarding private citizens owning and/or using guns. Our interest here is solely to remind our faithful warriors that they are no longer in a war zone and that possessing and using weapons is not a commonality in most civilian environs and situations.

4. Emotional control under pressure — not easily rattled and in control

Controlling emotions in combat vs. shut-down at home. ("It Don't Mean Nuthin'")

The Front = It was critical to control ("shut down") emotions for the sake of the mission. You were able to do the job while mastering strong feelings. Doing so made you a master of survival both emotionally and physically.

Home front hurdle:

The Home Front = Your loved ones expect to *see* emotions. Failing to express emotions may signal to those who mean the most to you that you don't care. You could come across as unloving and detached, (especially when you shut people out) and by doing so, damage many relationships. The lack of emotional connection is what destroys many relationships.

Recognize, renew, and redefine:

Capitalize on the strength that the emotional control you learned in the combat zone gave you. You performed many tasks while mastering strong emotions and it is this that can prove to be a powerful asset at home, especially when aggressive or angry feelings arise. Learn to feel again—both the good feelings and the not so good. Unthaw your heart and resume living.

Emotional control can also mean expressing emotions *as well as* holding them in. Remember...showing emotions is good for healthy relationships at home. *It is not a weakness!* ...Practice.

5. Disciplined and commanding presence

On the Front = Giving and taking orders is cut and dried. You were disciplined to receive and carry out orders. As someone with rank over other personnel you were disciplined to give orders and see that they were carried out...unwaveringly. Black and white thinking in the military kept you and others safe and in control of situations.

Home front hurdle:

On the Home Front = Inflexible mindsets (giving orders and making demands) often lead to conflict with loved ones, friends, in the workplace, etc. It may give you a reputation of being unapproachable and as a result, those around you will avoid interacting for fear of the consequences of being objectified.

Recognize, renew, and redefine:

Your family is not your military unit! Practice "middle ground." Negotiate. When you were deployed, time passed. Now be aware and acknowledge to yourself that your family may have developed new ways of doing things at home. You must learn to relax, observe, and appreciate this as growth...not something out of order, or something that you are not in control of. For those at home it was their way of forming some survival skills that got them through a difficult time during your absence.

Reflection and Review

~ Be prepared to negotiate: Negotiating for resolutions requires that you stop, wait, and listen...not bark orders. Practice walking in the other person's shoes (even your small children's shoes) to see their point of view the best you can. Middle ground techniques are good to learn and routinely practice—even though they do not come easy. It is this ability to empathize and negotiate that strengthens relationships.

CHAPTER TWELVE

MAKING IT HAPPEN...
TO THE REAR, MARCH!

Those years spent as a drill instructor has given me (Chuck) much to think about over the years. Taking average young Americans and turning them into combatants is not too difficult given the age-old training routines most militaries use. However, I have often wondered what it would take to help well-conditioned warriors return to conventional-thinking people once again. Can we provide tools for them to use to change back into people who automatically strive to resolve issues peacefully and productively? Is it possible for them to think differently, and not be so swift to revert to the combat mode as a first-option in handling situations? We believe that *re-training* our warriors to see the world not as a threat, but as a place where peace and logic accomplishes each "mission," heads you in the right direction to accomplish the mission of making better transitions upon coming home.

Bill Cosby coined the term "re-behaving", and our troops are now in dire need to learn the basics of re-behaving—to think and act as civilians once again. What they do, have done, or are now trained to do is *not* wrong—but many times their ingrained instinctual reactions do not fit into the new world back home as a civilian. We are convinced that one of our country's prime objectives should be to assist in this process. As a caring society we all need to lock arms and make this re-training a reality and priority in the transitional process.

Re-Behaving

Ready to rock and roll? It is time to do some matchmaking to help you re-behave.

There are some fun and productive ways to use your skills, education, and experiences; you need only to look back and examine what you now know. Remember…it took you countless hours to hone these skills while serving on military duty. We hope you can use these suggestions as a springboard to discover and develop your own personalized list. This is certainly not an exhaustive list of possibilities but perhaps it will give you some ideas to bounce off of while aligning your personal expertise with civilian endeavors.

A *military task description* is a phrase we have used to describe what you know and have become skilled at during military duty. It is not necessarily according to your military occupational specialty rating, but what you actually did and experienced while in the service. Here's how to make good use of your experiences:

Military task description

You became adept at living and functioning safely in exposed environments using your military training. (Field duty, bivouac, etc.)

Making it happen

Take your family camping and show them basic camping and survival skills. You can share your knowledge and impart valuable information to help them gain confidence in many areas of their lives. Another advantage (perhaps even more important for you) is the peace of mind it will give you knowing that your loved ones can better handle difficulties in life—especially in your absence. It will take the edge off and reduce any concern about your family's safety...which is a primary concern for most veterans once they get home.

Military task description

You were trained to function as a team member to accomplish missions. Even close order drill (marching as a unit, etc.), fire and maneuver exercises to assault a position as an infantryman requires the reliance of other unit members doing their jobs too in order to be a successful team.

Making it happen

As much as you tell yourself while on active duty that once you get out you will never stay in step with another person, or stand another inspection...please do not throw the baby out with the bathwater. Look for activities at work and pleasure that require you to participate as a member of a team. Staying in step in a marching formation was not just required so you would not step on the other guy. The procedures of teamwork were drilled into you so you would think "team"…and the mindset would become second nature. Use this skill now to enhance your lifestyle by seeking activities that accentuate this team attitude.

Military task description

Readiness and Inspections: There was a demand for you to be ready in season and out of season. If it was requested, you were trained to immediately answer the call and present your person, and/or equipment, for inspection to any senior person of authority.

Making it happen

Channel your training into helping your family develop harmony in the home and in your activities. Without conducting "inspections" to *demand* cleanliness, awareness, security, etc. you can be the tender warrior who sets examples and encourages positive improvements in your home-life. Your gentle and wise leadership will enhance personal growth in you and those around you.

Reflection and Review

~ Improving your life always takes a personal decision, but a decision is only as good as the information provided—and any subsequent action you take. Do a personal inventory again using the information from this chapter to help you follow through with some decisions. We hope you will find it useful in making a better redeployment back to civilian life.

CHAPTER THIRTEEN

OFF TO SEE THE WIZARD

Seeking help is not a sign of weakness.

In 2004, I (Bridget) was asked by the U.S. Army to provide mental health services to the paratroopers of the 173d Airborne Brigade stationed in Vicenza, Italy. While there, I focused on helping these troops reintegrate with their loved ones and readjust to peacetime conditions after their prolonged combat exposure in Northern Iraq.

I was well aware of the fact that many of the troopers were inclined to shy away from individual counseling due to a possible stigmatization seeing a "shrink" might bring. The fear of losing pride, position, rank, authority, employment, and a myriad of other important losses, came as a result of the PTSD survivor thinking that seeking help for emotional burdens was a sign of weakness. This is not so, and I can only hope that this myth changes soon for the good of our warriors and their families.

Knowing this I tried to conduct as many *group* sessions as possible, and on three different occasions I spoke to battalion-size groups. This worked well because I was able to impart many specifics about war stress, and offer good tools without anyone feeling threatened or picked on. The individual sessions I was able to have were enlightening and much good came from them as well. However, more could have been done in this arena had the "stigma" not been there.

Over the years I have counseled veterans from all walks of life. Some have held positions of high responsibility such as police officers, paramedics, business owners, and current military NCOs and Officers. When it is suggested that they "talk to someone," the same stigma raises its head, and many hesitate far too long to ask for (and/or get) the help they so desperately need.

While in Italy I worked closely with the Chaplains of the Brigade. They were wonderful men and warriors in their own right. As the days went by I did notice an interesting dynamic among the troops and chaplains that is worth mentioning, and it may be an answer for those who feel nervous about seeking professional help for stress management.

Many of the troops indicated that if they made an appointment to see a mental health practitioner or the Army stress team, they would be publicly *admitting* they had issues which could have detrimental connotations. But making an appointment to speak with a chaplain is a different story. The paratroopers felt it was safer because a person can have dozens of reasons to see a chaplain, and thereby maintain a different level of confidentiality. Perhaps that bit of information will help you get onto a good and healthy route if there is something that needs attending to. Seeking out a Chaplain to talk to could also be an easier runway to finally receiving professional counseling. The Chaplain can make a referral for additional support.

The End is the Beginning

Keep in mind that the ending to this book is just the beginning—Once you have read it, it is time to start. Starting is often one of the most challenging steps to take during transitions, but to make it work you must begin somewhere.

Here are some thoughts and tips I will offer as a mental health professional. I hope they will direct you to some good decisions in seeking the help that best suits you.

First of all, listen to yourself and to those around you. Those close to you can serve as a good "temperature gauge" to see how you are handling situations at home and in your civilian environment. Recognizing and admitting that things are not going as you had envisioned is the first step towards your journey from warrior to civilian.

Next you need to know that some of the first signs of distress are the sleepless nights, the anger, and the unsettling feelings that just eat at your gut. Something is just not right and you cannot figure out what it is. You may feel edgy and impatient and act in ways which are disturbing and unfamiliar to you in the home environment. This is an indication you are beginning to recognize personal changes that have occurred while you were away.

You have learned valuable military skills which were vital for your survival and for those around you. You developed confidence in being able to carry out a mission and make it back home. Now, however, you may discover life is different— You are different. It is not uncommon to feel as if you need to once again be with the men and women you served with but for the most part this is impossible. At this point it is time to make the best of your situation and decide to take on a new mission of *relearning* how to live in peace and harmony with those at home. You need to make a quality decision to take those skills and experiences you have honed, now utilize them and put them to good use in a positive and productive way.

One caveat is that your new mission will not be accomplished overnight; you may fall and bang your knees many times along the way. However, take some comfort in this: There are many good people at home who are here to help pick you up, blow off the dirt and tell you "it's going to be okay, you're going to make it." Welcome home.

Reflection and Review

~ Being honest and acknowledging that PTSD and/ or COS is an emotional challenge, but *not* a sign of weakness, is a major step in the right direction.

~ You are not alone in this process and many of your comrades are dealing with these issues as well. Here are facts that may help you to understand more:

According to the PDRHL from the Department of Defense Behavioral Health Survey 43% of 2000 National Guard Members had readjustment issues after returning from the war zone(s). Nationally, the overall rate of PTSD has been described as being at *least* 30%.

With early intervention (unlike the warriors in other conflicts who preceded you) the duration of PTSD symptoms are reduced from 64 months to 36 months.

In regards to *stigmas* from obtaining mental health services, here are some very fascinating statistics:

According to Hoge, et al. 2004, the following are statements that were grouped and analyzed to point out the beliefs underlying barriers to seeking out professional help.

(*Reflect and review* where you are positioned in regards to these attitudes.)

I would be seen as weak by my unit members 65%
My unit leadership might treat me differently 63%
My unit would have less confidence in me   59%
My leaders would blame me for the problem 51%
It would harm my career   50%
Difficulty getting time off work for treatment 55%
It is difficult to schedule an appointment   45%
I don't trust mental health professionals   38%
Mental health care doesn't work   25%
I don't know where to get help   22%

~ There are certainly other reasons not mentioned that may stand in the way of men and women in uniform getting the help they need. It is our hope you will make your own determination and realize how critical it is to be pro-active to get the help you need and deserve. The outcome for a better adjustment is now in your hands.

CHAPTER FOURTEEN

FROM RIFLE TO RELATIONSHIP
~COUPLES CONNECTING~

No book on transitioning from warrior to civilian is complete without a punctuating note regarding relationships.

All humans need nurturing, loving, and supportive relationships with others. There are overwhelming physical, social, financial, and psychological advantages for people who have healthy relationships. In hundreds of studies researchers have found many benefits in those subjects who had positive relationships.

Therefore, while researchers continue to document the positive benefits of healthy relationships, it is our focus to help warriors and their partners strengthen ties with one another. After many years of failing in the relationship department, I (Chuck) can speak from experience.

In the summer of 1963 my life changed forever. I was no longer "Chuck Dean the civilian." I was now a mere number in a long green line of other Army recruits. I finished sixteen weeks of U.S. Army basic and advanced training early in the spring and then at the hottest time of the year, I was off to Fort Benning, Georgia to see if I could make it as a paratrooper. I could have chosen an easier way to spend my Army enlistment; instead I volunteered to jump out of perfectly good airplanes. This meant I had to pay my dues by completing a grueling training course designed to weed out the weakest and validate the strongest.

My class for the jump school started with a little over 1100 men, and at the end of 5 weeks only 650 graduated. Still marveling that I had lasted, I'll never forget the day I stood on that dusty parade field having silver wings pinned on me by the very man who nearly killed me with physical torture for all those weeks. Every man standing in that parade formation knew we could now live up to our class motto, "The best above the rest," and we were now expected to live and fight according to that standard.

I volunteered for a couple of personal reasons. First of all it challenged me with a desire to serve with America's finest fighting men, a "brotherhood of the best," and if I could make the grade, I would be part of an elite *family* while serving my country. Second, jumping from airplanes meant honor, respect, physical well-being, and doing my best as a better way of getting through the Army.

I wanted to make my service time a positive, challenging experience, but deep inside what I really longed for was to belong to something greater than me. The paratroops gave me that. It gave me a *family* that would be like-minded and focused; a group of individuals serving together to maintain cohesiveness and unit integrity. It was a unit that would not quit on me.

Boot Camp Family Maker

A few years later, after a tour in Vietnam, I returned to the U.S. and was assigned to Fort Ord, California to serve as a drill instructor for basic infantry training. Here again I was challenged, but in a different way. It was my job to turn undisciplined, individual civilians into units of men who could march in step and sing the same cadence songs. My assignment was to get them to march to the same drumbeat, and be a team…a *family*.

As perfect strangers they were lined up and made into this family. These young men from day-one bunked together, showered together, hurt together, and overcame together. I took individuals with slack attitudes and systematically changed them into soldiers who took seriously the matters of serving as a team in uniform. They became men who depended on one another to pass inspections, master tactics, and provide protection for each other. They became committed to working as a unit in order to accomplish goals and succeed in whatever they were ordered to do. These several individuals became one entity—They learned to live and work together to get things done. They may have had disagreements and fights among themselves, and at times they thought they hated each other, but if ever another platoon degraded or came against one in my platoon, they came against all 32 of my men. I have seen this same dynamic happen in many families, including my own.

My emphasis as a drill instructor who had served in a combat zone was not necessarily to train troops in military courtesy, saluting, parade-ground drills, or spit and polish. I had other priorities. I did expect my trainees to learn all those military qualities, but I knew where they were going and I wanted them to come home alive. I made sure they learned the more important aspects of surviving warfare.

In the short 8-week basic infantry training course my focus was primarily on two areas: (1) weapons training and maintenance, and (2) first aid. They needed to know their weapons inside and out and to be proficient in firing them, and they needed to know how to save their buddy's life if he got hit in combat. Consequently, with each training cycle my platoons always scored high in marksmanship and first aid on their final examinations.

From Rifle to Relationship

A rifle was issued to each soldier. It had a serial number on it and each man was accountable for its condition as long as it was assigned to him. He was expected to care for that weapon as gently as he would his partner. He slept with his rifle. He cleaned it, and he stood inspection with it. Each soldier became familiar with every part of that assigned weapon. He could take it apart and re-assemble it blindfolded, and learned how to fire and adjust it according to his own sight patterns.

Relationships are no different and one could consider the relationship with a partner as a "weapon", in a good sense in that a weapon is an essential part of survival. He (or she) can be a comforting weapon to have in an arsenal if recognized and respected. So let's see how this connects.

In the military we are issued a weapon and we have no choices. However, in civilian life we do when selecting a suitable partner in order to establish a healthy and loving relationship.

It is our responsibility to account for and nurture our relationships. In a similar way we must make sure they are in working order and properly maintained.

It behooves us to care for our relationships the same as we did our weapons while on active duty. In the military we learn to live with our weapon. We eat with it, sleep with it and will be in big trouble should we lose it. It becomes an interesting part of intimacy. Can you see how this also relates to healthy intimacy in your relationships?

I remember having my trainees stand morning inspection before another day on the rifle range. Some would fall into formation with mud still in their flash suppressor from the training the day before and others would have well-oiled and clean weapons. What was in the difference?

For eight grueling weeks these trainees had no time for themselves and very little time to accomplish what was expected of them in preparation for the next day. When the lights go out at 9 pm and you have arrived back to barracks from a night problem at 7 pm, you have choices to make. You know your rifle and equipment are still muddy and grimy, and you barely have time to breathe a relaxed breath before the next day starts all over again. So, the lights go out and the rifle needs to get cleaned; you can choose to clean the weapon in the dark or lay it aside and say "forget it, I'll face the consequences." It really boiled down to who was going to do the job in spite of the conditions. The conditions in relationships are not always optimum, and when those conditions become confusing and stressful, you have the choice to either handle the situation, or turn out the lights and hope it will go away on its own. From experience most of us can vouch that it does not *just* go away, but will usually worsen if left alone.

The next translated thought from "rifle to relationship" is familiarization.

When two people come together and form a relationship, the first thing they do is figure one another out. They usually begin to find out what makes the other person "tick."

Military trainees are expected to know their weapon inside and out. They must be able to field strip their weapon (break it down to the smallest part) and put it back together in the most adverse conditions…dark being the worst. When we become involved with another person, the first thing we need to do is exactly that. It is important to identify the make up of the other person piece by piece. When we become confused and frustrated in a relationship, it is critical that we know how to pick up the essential pieces of the relationship and put them back the way we found them — the way it was supposed to be.

After my trainees were issued rifles, they were sent to the range and began their weapons indoctrination. One of the first phases of this training was to "zero" their rifles. This was adjusting the sights to their individual vision.

The targets that they fired at to zero were only 25 meters away, and to be "zeroed" the trainee had to fire three rounds into a three-round shot pattern the size of a quarter. When he could do that, his rifle was adjusted to hit targets up to 1000 meters away.

Everyone sees a target differently and each rifle has to be calibrated for that difference. If a trainee's rifle is not zeroed to his sight, then his aim will be off, and his marksmanship will be severely hindered. He will not be able hit targets at any distance in order to qualify with the weapon.

It is very similar when we set our sights on having a relationship. Our sights must be adjusted to that particular person. We cannot hit the target if we think or act in random and general terms that do not address specific needs. Every person is different and when we choose to be in a relationship, it is essential that we adjust our vision (and thinking) to align with those of the person with whom we have a relationship. If we do not, we will miss targets at every distance, and fail to accomplish our goals.

Reflection and Review

~ There are two kinds of relationships: (1) Life-giving relationships and (2) Life-consuming relationships. It is important to decide which kind you are involved in and if you are not giving "life" to your relationship, you must determine what responsibility you and your partner need to take in order to give it the life it deserves.

CHAPTER FIFTEEN

PARTNERS ON THE HOME FRONT

In our research we have found it necessary, and of great importance, to help those folks waiting on the home front to be prepared and become more aware of what to expect when their warrior comes home.

For the partner or family member living with a person who has PTSD or COS, it is important to be supportive without completely losing your identity or sense of self. You can actually be a "second set of eyes" by heightening your awareness and increasing your empathy, so that you can understand how your loved one is being affected by the symptoms of stress. Being aware of your partner's triggers is important to building trust and intimacy in the relationship. It is important for your warrior to feel supported and loved. The chances of this happening are better if the partner or family member understands what is involved in the transition journey from warrior to civilian.

Each warrior *knows* that he or she will be challenged in readjusting upon his or her return. Being well equipped to support them will make all the difference in how well that transition goes.

How will it be Different?

It is impossible to say exactly how your loved one will be when he or she returns. Everyone has a different resiliency and toleration level to hardships. We can, however, give you a combination of signs along the trail, "red-flag" warnings, and some actual experiences from veterans of earlier wars to help you understand and be better prepared for the homecoming.

Change: Listed below are some ways that we have seen returnees change because of the exposure to the hardships and dangers of war. Some of these changes may seem unreal to you, but if your loved one is reacting to them, they are issues to be recognized and dealt with.

Your warrior:

◆ Is now quiet and over-reflective (almost as if not present).
◆ Is now nervous and jumpy at the slightest provocation.
◆ Is now overly sensitive to sights, sounds, and situations that are reminders of the war zone.
◆ Is now short-tempered and becomes easily frustrated or angry over seemingly small matters.
◆ Cannot tolerate simple mistakes made by those around him or her.
◆ Cannot remain in crowds or social gatherings for any length of time. Is always looking for a way out.

Quirks/habits: Your warrior may have developed some quirks or habits as a means to physically survive or care for oneself emotionally while in the war zone.

Your warrior may:

♦ Have a "defensive "perimeter wire" in place and cannot allow anyone to get too close. (This could be a result of subconscious vows not to allow anyone too close because it is too painful when you lose them.)
♦ Sleep with the lights on all night.
♦ Sleep with weapons.
♦ Sit in "strategic" places in public places to detect and be alert for sudden enemy attacks.
♦ Not want to unpack the clothes brought back from the war zone. (Too many reminders are in the duffle bag, or he or she may have the feeling they will be called back and need to have things packed and ready at a moment's notice.)

What You can do to Prepare:

The very first thing you need to do is prepare yourself mentally for the changes and differences that will prevail for a while in your relationship. As much as we all want things to go back to the way they were *before* deployment, you come to realize this is an unreal expectation. To think that you and your loved can go back to square one and pick up where you left off is setting yourself up for a loss and disappointment. Time has passed and lives have changed. Be progressive and stay focused in the here and now. Here are some ways to prepare.

◆ For couples: Plan to start the dating process all over again. Rekindle the friendship and romantic aspects of your relationship, and sort out the responsibilities afterwards.

◆ For family members: Plan to view the relationship in the present and avoid trying to re-live childhood activities, remembrances, and/or dreams. (After engaging in wartime activities, dreams and innocent notions of life may have been shattered and most likely the furthest thing from one's mind. Bringing the memories of their past life can remind them too much of what they have lost.)

◆ Plan ways to be sensitive to your loved one's idiosyncrasies. For example, it is considerate to ask them where *they* would like to sit in a restaurant. Refrain from demanding that they go shopping in crowded malls. Do what you can to keep the kids from crawling on them too much (remember the "perimeter wire?"). Do not take it personally if your loved one does not hug as much as you would like. If you give them space by understanding and respecting the "wire" principle, they are likely to draw closer over time.

How Can Home Front Partners Prepare their Children?

Children will have understandable fears for the safety of parents sent overseas. It is important for you, the parent or family member, to know what to expect in children while their loved one is deployed. You can prepare the child first and foremost by educating yourself on spotting and dealing with their potential reactions to the new experience. It is crucial to provide an opportunity for children to discuss their concerns and to help them separate real from imagined fears. It is also important to limit exposure to media coverage of violence, or news topics related to the military.

Parents and relatives at home can help by letting children honestly express feelings and concerns. Frequent telephone calls, letters and/or email are essential in helping children feel connected to, and loved by, absent parents. Because repeated scenes of destruction of lives and property are featured in the daily news media, they may understand that "enemies of the United States" can harm their loved one. We adults need to help children feel encouraged and safe at a time when the world seems to be a more dangerous place. As much as possible we need to carry their share of the worry and pain that war causes. It is our duty to lift the weight from their shoulders.

We were once standing in an art display of very graphic Vietnam War scenes when a young mother came through leading a small boy of perhaps 4 years old. She was curious and wanted to take in what she could without spending a lot of time exposing her son to the impacting scenes. As she hastily dragged the boy along, he suddenly pointed at one of the paintings and asked, "Momma, what is that?" What she said next remains with us as something very profound. She wisely answered him, "Someday you'll know, but for now I'll carry that load so you won't have to." She hurriedly exited the display and went about being a protective mom.

Emotional Responses:

Emotional responses vary in nature and severity from child to child. Nonetheless, there are some similarities in how children feel when their lives are impacted by war or the threat of war:

◆ *Fear:* Fear may be the predominant reaction—fear for the safety of those in the military. When children hear rumors at school and pick up bits of information from television, their imaginations may run wild. They may think the worst, so it is important to monitor and explain what is happening.

◆ *Loss of control:* Military actions are something over which children—and most adults—have no control. Lack of control can be overwhelming and confusing. Children may grasp at any control that they have, including refusing to cooperate, go to school, part with favorite toys, or leave your side. This need to be in "control" of their environment may linger long after the deployed parents return home.

◆ *Anger:* Anger is a common reaction and may often be a substitute (or familiar emotion) to express sadness or loss. Unfortunately, anger is often expressed at those to whom children are closest. Children may direct anger toward classmates and neighbors because they cannot express their anger toward those responsible for their parents being sent to war. Some children may show unexpected anger toward parents who are at home or those in the military, even to the extent that they do not want to write letters or draw pictures or send gifts. (This could be the child's way of developing his or her own "perimeter wire.") Even after the parent returns, the child may be distant and disconnected.

◆ *Loss of stability:* War or military deployment interrupts routines. It is unsettling. Children can feel insecure when their usual schedules and activities are disrupted, which increases their level of stress and need for reassurance. Even the adults are dealing with their own instability, and children are easily influenced by their environment.

It is important to use good judgment in your daily behavior, and not burden your child with your emotional
pain. Do your best to be upbeat and cheerful, and make
time to be with your children.

◆ *Isolation:* Children who have a family member in the
military but who do not live near a military base may
feel more isolated. Children of reserve members called
to active duty may not know others in the same situation. Such children may feel resentment and sadness
toward friends whose families are intact (not deployed).
They may strike out at signs of normalcy around them.
Another group of children who may feel isolated are
dependents of military families who have accompanied
a remaining parent back to a hometown, or who are
staying with relatives while both parents are gone. Not
only do these children experience separation anxiety
from parents, but they also experience the loss of familiar faces and surroundings. Their world is no longer
predictable and this can cause much anxiety.

◆ *Confusion:* This can occur on two levels. First, children
may feel confused about the concept of war and what
further dangers might arise. Second, children may have
trouble understanding the difference between violence
as entertainment and the real events taking place on
the news. Today's children live in the world of *Armaged-
don, Independence Day, Air Force One,* and cartoon Super
Heroes. Some of the modern media violence is
unnervingly real. Youngsters may have difficulty sepa-
rating reality from fantasy, cartoon heroes, and villains,
from the government soldiers and real terrorists. Sepa-
rating the realities of war from media fantasy does
require adult help. Be careful to monitor programs and
video games. Observe their reactions and be prepared
to answer questions.

What Can Parents Do?

Everyone, including adults, feels stress during times of crisis and uncertainty. If your children seem to need help beyond what is normally available at home or school, seek mental health services in your community. Psychologists, counselors and social workers can identify issues and provide appropriate support and help with the referral process. For most children, adults can provide adequate support by the following actions:

Acknowledge children's feelings:

◆ Knowing what to say is often difficult. When no other words come to mind, a hug and saying "This is really hard for you/us" will help, but giving them an avenue of positive re-direction by engaging them in a stimulating activity will do wonders.

◆ Try to recognize the feelings underlying children's actions and put them into words. Say something like, "I can see you have feelings about this. Tell me more about them." Be careful not tell your children how *they* are feeling; instead, let them tell you. A very good technique to express emotion is through art, music, and acting. Invite the child to use these methods to physically demonstrate his or her feelings. (Younger children may find that using these alternative modes of communication are easier ways to express themselves.)

◆ Sometimes children may voice concern about what will happen to them if a parent does not return. If this occurs, offer something like this, "You will be well taken care of. You won't be alone. What would this look like to you if this happened? Let me tell you our plan and we can work together." Reassure both the younger and older child that you have a plan that will take care of them.

♦ At times when your children are most upset, do not deny the seriousness of the situation. Saying to children, "Don't cry, everything will be okay," does not reflect how the child feels and does not make them feel better. Nevertheless, do not forget to express hope and faith that things will be okay; remember to be truthful with what is appropriate for the age and situation. Determine whether or not your own fears are being projected onto your child. Remember...it is not appropriate for your children to carry your burden as well as their own.

♦ Older children, in particular, may require help clarifying what they believe about war and the role of the United States in this current conflict. They may ask some very poignant questions which you need to be prepared to address. "Will my parent kill someone?" and "Are we killing innocent people in other countries?" are questions that may need discussion. It may be a time to speak to a clergy person and discuss the morality of war. Perhaps it is also good to remind the children that we hope our military can do enough to stop the war and help bring peace in other countries.

♦ Always be honest with children. Share your fears and concerns with discretion, while at the same time reassuring them that responsible adults are in charge.

♦ If participation in a faith community is part of your family life, talk to your faith leader about how to help your child think about and process the concepts of death and killing, in age-appropriate terms. This can be very important to calming your fear, as well as those of your children.

◆ Try to maintain normal routines and schedules to provide a sense of stability and security within the family, school and your community.

Help children maintain a sense of control by taking some action:

◆ Send letters, cookies or magazines to those in the military.
◆ Help older children find a family who has a parent on active duty and arrange some volunteer babysitting times for that family or offer to provide meals occasionally. These types of activities and support are vital for feeling a sense of purpose and community that can serve as healthy and productive expressions of compassion.

If a family member is away, make plans for some special activities:

◆ Gatherings with other families who have a loved one on active duty can help provide support for you as well as for your children.
◆ Special parent and child times can provide an extra sense of security, which might be needed. Let your child know that you will set aside a particular half hour each day to play. Make the time as pleasant and child-centered as possible. Return phone calls later and make your child the real focus of that special time.
◆ Organize a consistent pattern, which ensures a child of positive expectations, such as regular meal times. Morning and bedtime rituals (bathing, prayer, reading stories, etc.) can provide a wonderful sense of peace and security for both parent and child.

◆ Involve children in planning how to cope. Control and ownership are fostered when children help to plan strategies for dealing with a situation. Children often have practical and creative ideas for coping. Be open and willing to adjust your life accordingly. Be flexible without losing a sense of control.

Expect and respond to changes in behavior:

◆ All children will likely display some signs of stress. Some immature, aggressive, oppositional, as well as regressive, withdrawn and isolative behaviors are reactions to the uncertainty of this situation. We advise that you seek professional help if these behaviors continue. Just by having an objective third party to intervene can make a big difference in the well-being of your child's mental health.

◆ Even though there is a significant shift in the family structure, it is important to maintain consistent expectations for behavior. Be sure children understand that the same rules apply that were in place prior to the change. Maintain routines.

◆ It is important that the roles remain intact. You do not want to undermine this principle by imposing a false authority upon a child. For example, one of the most damaging expectations, or "assignments," is to say, "Your dad is gone to war, so now you're the man of the house." This does not work. It confuses the child who may now see this status as an added obligation and burden to uphold. On the other hand, the child may not be so willing to relinquish this title when the parent returns to his place in the family.

◆ Some children whose parents are on active duty may have difficulty at bedtime. Maintain a regular bedtime routine. Be flexible about nightlights, siblings sharing a room, sleeping with special toys, and sitting with your child as he or she falls asleep. Doing so typically does not cause life-long habits. These are comforting means to provide reassurance to a child.

Extra support, consistency, empathy and patience will help children return to routines and their more usual behavior patterns. If children show extreme reactions (aggression, withdrawal, sleeping problems, etc.), consult with a mental health professional regarding the symptoms of severe stress and keep communication open.

Keep adult issues from overwhelming children:

◆ Do not let your children focus too much of their time and energy on the situation of having a loved one at war. If children are choosing to watch the news for hours each evening, find other activities for them. You may also need to watch the news less intensely and spend more time in alternative family activities.
◆ Know the facts about developments in the war. Be prepared to answer your children's questions factually, and take time to think about how you want to frame events and your reactions to them.
◆ Try not to let financial strains be a major concern of children. For National Guard or Reserve families, going from a civilian job to active duty in the military may cut family income. Children are not capable of dealing with this issue on an ongoing basis. Telling a

child that you need to be more careful with spending is appropriate, but be cautious about placing major burdens on them.

♦ And finally...self-care. Take time for yourself and try to deal with your own reactions to the situation as fully as possible. This, too, will help your child's well-being. You need to be the rock.

Home Front Partner Self-Care:

When the oxygen mask drops out of the ceiling on airplanes, adults are instructed to place their masks on themselves before doing the same for any small children near them. It takes no explanation to see why this sequence is vital to survival. Likewise, it is a perfect illustration of why your *self-care* is so important. If you are not taking care of yourself properly, it is unlikely that your family will get the best care from you either. Only when we first help ourselves can we effectively help others. Caring for yourself is one of the most important—and one of the most often forgotten—things you can do as a parent who is carrying the load while a loved one is deployed. When *your* needs are taken care of, the person you care for will benefit as well.

When it comes to surviving the deployment of a loved one, you must do what you can to nurture yourself both physically and emotionally. This can be a difficult task since you are now standing in for both sides of the parenting spectrum, and have many more responsibilities to tend to than before.

In conclusion we invite you to reflect upon and review the following tips and guidelines that may help you focus on this self-care procedure. These are a few ideas that you can try that may help you put special attention on yourself.

Reflection and Review

~Tips for home front partner self-care:
- Learn and use stress-reduction techniques. (Relaxation, deep breathing, etc.)
- Attend to your own healthcare needs and implement a vitamin program.
- Get proper rest and nutrition.
- Exercise regularly.
- Take time off without feeling guilty.
- Participate in pleasant, nurturing activities with other grown-ups.
- Seek and accept the support of others. Spend time each day conversing (in person, phone, or e-mail) with another supportive adult who can share your burden.
- Seek supportive counseling when you need it, or talk to a trusted counselor or friend.
- Identify and acknowledge your feelings.
- Begin to view situations in a more positive way. Look for the good—not the bad.
- Take up a personal hobby.
- Limit your exposure to, and use of, alcohol and drugs.
- Set goals. (Take baby steps on this and you will be fine).

As we come to a close we encourage you to stay in touch with us. We welcome your feedback on this book and other materials that we have compiled to help warriors and their families make good transitions. Please feel free to contact the authors about any part of this book.

To order additional copies, including bulk order discount prices, please write, call or e-mail:

Hearts Toward Home International
1050 Larrabee Avenue
Suite 104, PMB 714
Bellingham, Washington 98225-7367
(360) 714-1525 extension #2
Website: www.heartstowardhome.com

REFERENCE SUGGESTIONS

The following are some books that we recommend for partners and loved ones of warriors. Each book has a website from where they can be ordered.

"Once a Warrior: Wired for Life" Workbook Course, Bridget C. Cantrell, Ph.D. and Chuck Dean

"Down Range: To Iraq and Back" Bridget C. Cantrell, Ph.D. and Chuck Dean

"Turning Your Hearts Toward Home" Workbook Course, Bridget C. Cantrell, Ph.D. with Chuck Dean
www.heartstowardhome.com
(Hearts Toward Home International is a non-profit, charitable organization designed to assist veterans and families in making positive transitions after wartime experiences. The founder, Dr. Bridget C. Cantrell conducts lectures, workshops, and training seminars on an international level to help facilitate transitioning troops, their leaders, and their families. Her focus centers on helping both war veterans and family members alike discover and resolve the core issues that work against healthy reconnections after wartime experiences. Hearts Toward Home International exists for the purpose of providing support, counseling, training, educational classes, materials, and re-integration and re-adjustment workshop/forums for military personnel (both active duty and veterans) and their families after war-time service.)

"When the War is Over: A New One Begins" Chuck Dean and Bette Nordberg
www.namvetbook.com

REFERENCE SUGGESTIONS

"Nam Vet: Making Peace with Your past" Chuck Dean
www.namvetbook.com

"Heroes at Home: Help and Hope for America's Military Families" Ellie Kay
www.bethanyhouse.com

"Solo Ops: A Survival Guide for Military Wives" Hilary Martin
Orders@Xlibris.com

"Surviving Deployment: A Guide for Military Families" Karen Pavlicin
www.amazon.com

THE AUTHORS
~ Recipients of the
Didi Hirsch Community Mental Health
2008 Erasing the Stigma Leadership Award ~

Bridget C. Cantrell, Ph.D.

Dr. Bridget C. Cantrell is a member of the American Psychological Association and Association of Traumatic Stress Specialists. With a Ph.D. in Clinical Psychology, she is a licensed Mental Health Counselor in the State of Washington, and a Nationally Board Certified Mental Health Counselor. She currently works as one of a small number of specially selected and trained Washington State Department of Veterans Affairs Post-Traumatic Stress Disorder (PTSD) Specialists.

Dr. Cantrell currently is the President/CEO of Hearts Toward Home International, a charitable non-profit organization dedicated to the recovery and reintegration of trauma survivors. Hearts Toward Home International was recognized as the 2008 Best of Bellingham Award in the Non-profit Charitable Organization category by the U.S. Local Business Association (USLBA).

For nearly two decades Dr. Cantrell has provided therapeutic counseling for war veterans and their families. Presently, she provides mental health services to active duty troops from all branches of the military, including Reservists, National Guard, their leaders and family members. This work focuses on providing effective tools for military personnel to readjust after experiencing the impact of combat exposure, trauma, family deployment stress and many other readjustment issues as a result of service overseas.

Dr. Cantrell travels extensively teaching and lecturing throughout the European and Pacific duty assignments. She is headquartered in Bellingham, Washington.

Chuck Dean

In early 1987, Chuck Dean, a veteran of the Vietnam War, became the Executive Director of Point Man International, a veterans-for-veterans support organization. As a writer and counselor he has worked with thousands of soldiers and veterans not only in the United States, but several foreign countries—including Russia, Italy, and France. His mission, born from his own experiences, has always been to see other veterans find positive solutions to the many issues facing them upon returning from combat.

He has worked extensively in the publishing industry, and is the author of several books on recovery issues, such as *"Nam Vet: Making Peace with Your Past"* and *"When the War is Over".* His latest work, *"Down Range: To Iraq and Back",* and *"Once a Warrior: And Wired for Life"* are written and designed with critical transitional information for the current military and veterans. Both books are co-authored with Bridget C. Cantrell, Ph.D.

Chuck spent six years in the U.S. Army as a paratrooper in the 82nd Airborne Division, and the 173d Airborne Brigade in Vietnam and Okinawa. He was one of the first 300 regular Army troops to be deployed to S.E. Asia in 1965. Upon his return from the combat zone, he spent two years as a Drill Instructor at Ft. Ord, California. Later Chuck served eight years as the National Chaplain for the 173d Airborne Brigade Association. He and his wife, Jingwen, live in the Pacific Northwest.